SORRY

The Gifts of Confession and Forgiveness

LIN BUTTON

To Ron, my husband and fellow traveller on the journey of living life to the full.

CONTENTS

ACKNOWLEDGEMENTS

To Anne, Ellie and Sheila, my friends with whom I discovered the gift of confession.

To the Monday Group

The women with whom I practice loving God, others and myself. The place where we try to be authentic.

To the Healing Prayer School Team

The group where we listen to God's word and grow together in knowledge and love.

Special thanks to

Pamela Evans, Jean Godlonton, Becky Harcourt and Geoff Hodgkins for proof reading, grammar corrections and for all the helpful comments.

Vivienne Stockley for typing my lectures, assisting with researching and her unique, joyful way of helping me.

Anita Henser for her typing, re-typing and organizing of the printing of this book alongside her administration of conferences, producing CD's and creating the website.

INTRODUCTION

Sorry Matters

'Confess your sins to one another that you may be healed.'
(James 5:16 NIV)

Sorry Matters explores the gifts of confession and forgiveness and names some of the barriers to receiving the gift.

Chapter One looks at where it all went wrong in the Garden of Eden and how that led to shame and hiding.

Chapter four is an attempt to look at how we get stuck in suffering. It is not intended to offer all of the answers to suffering but more to how a different attitude can help bring change.

Chapters five and six are about the actual gifts. The picture I had in my mind whilst writing this book was doing the first four chapters to unwrap the gifts.

Chapter seven is intended as a 'hope' section of how life can be.

This book is the third in the series 'Changing Lives' and as such is a companion to Father Matters and Mother Matters.

I hope it blesses you to read it as much as it has blessed me to write it.

Lin Button

1

'*In the beginning when God created the heavens and the earth*'(Genesis 1:1) He made something wondrous - beautiful.

Now, we only have glimpses of the place God made for us to live in. Sometimes we stand looking at the beauty of mountains, or a waterfall, a glorious sunset or the early first light of dawn promising a new day - the occasional rainbow causing our hearts to remember God's everlasting covenant.

> '*I have placed my rainbow in the clouds. It is the sign of my permanent promise to you and to all the earth. When I send clouds over the earth, the rainbow will be seen in the clouds, and I will remember my covenant with you and with everything that lives. Never again will there be a flood that will destroy all life. When I see the rainbow in the clouds, I will remember the eternal covenant between God and every living creature on earth.*' (Genesis 9:13-16)

The Bible teaches that everything and everyone was created by God. As C.S Lewis says, 'No philosophical theory which I have yet come across is a radical improvement on the words of Genesis. In the beginning God made Heaven and earth.' [1]

God spoke as the Creator-King announcing His crowning work. Having rubbed the stardust off His hands He said, 'Let us make man.'

> 'Then God said, "Let us make people in our image, to be like ourselves. They will be masters over all life, the fish in the sea, the birds in the sky and all the livestock, wild animals and small animals."'(Genesis 1:26)

Man is the climax of God's creative activity and God has 'crowned him with glory and honour.' (Psalm 8) This glory and honour is often marred by sin but all mankind is made in the image of God and carries something of His image within, although in a 'broken', 'shattered' or 'hidden' state.

So, we were all created in the image of God, fearfully and wonderfully made, fashioned as living icons. As G. K. Chesterton said, 'We were statues of God walking about in a garden.' [2] In

'*The Message*' it says that God created human beings '*God-like*.'

(Genesis 1:27)

Paraphrasing C. S. Lewis: 'If we saw ourselves as we really

were we'd be tempted to kneel down and worship ourselves.'[3]

We were endowed with strength and beauty all of our own;

we were fully alive. Our original glory came before our sin and is

therefore deeper to our nature. We hear a lot about original sin

but little about us as masterpieces created by God. Often we

know of someone without any apparent faith acting selflessly,

even heroically in times of crisis. It would appear that someone

far away from God hears something of His whisper. God's image

remains deep within the person.

Knowing that we are created by God we need to accept

ourselves because, as human beings, we have been given

infinite worth.

When God says let us make man in our image this doesn't mean God created us exactly the same as Himself. We are reflectors of God's glory.

There's great debate as to why the plural 'us' refers to God at this climactic moment of creation. The discussion is whether it is God and a heavenly Council or the persons of the Trinity. Another view states that the plural wording is used to denote majesty. Today many kings and queens will still use the plural form when speaking of themselves. Or, indeed, is the image of God in which humankind is created intentionally, obscured? There are no definite answers to these questions but what is absolutely clear is that within this vast creation story God wants human company and conversation.

God is complete within Himself and although He doesn't need us He does want us to be co-workers.

In poetic language, I like the idea of the love between the Trinity being so great that it spilled over into the creation of the world. We could then say we were the 'love child' of the Trinity. Adam and Eve were in partnership with God encountering Him face-to-face. They were naked and unashamed, God conscious rather than self-conscious, living together with God where they were able to know and be known. This is God's intention for us - as we live in the knowledge of our inheritance and who God created us to be. He wants us to learn how to live in intimacy - 'into-me-see.'

The completion of all that God created culminates in His relationship with us human creatures. And God proclaims this very good.

'Then God looked over all he had made, and he saw that it was excellent in every way! And evening passed and morning came. This all happened on the sixth day.'
(Genesis 1:31)

One of the challenges of the Bible is for us to believe what God says about us. Having declared us very good in our original creation, or blueprint for our lives, the truth of His continual affirmation of how He sees us and loves us is something we find difficult to grasp. For instance, do we really believe we are the *'apple of God's eye?'* (Zechariah 2:8)

And do we really understand what a glorious inheritance we have? Where do we come from? Children often ask this question. We as adults like to know our family tree and watch TV programmes like 'Who Do You Think You Are?' making a strong link between family and identity.

The 'who am I'? and 'where did I come from'? questions mean our spiritual heart is never fully satisfied until we find God. St. Augustine said, 'Our hearts are restless until they find their rest in Thee.'[4]

C. S. Lewis writes:

'Apparently, then, our lifelong nostalgia, our longing to be reunited with something in the universe from which we now feel cut off, to be on the inside of some door which we have always seen from the outside, is no mere neurotic fancy, but the truest index of our real situation. And to be at last summoned inside would be both glory and honour beyond all our merits and also the healing of that old ache.'[5]

What both St. Augustine and C. S. Lewis are illustrating is something deep within our nature. We are all 'Homesick for Eden.'

So where did it all go wrong? How did we end up 'homeless' with feelings of isolation, shame, guilt and fear?

Lurking in the Garden was an enemy forced out of heaven but not destroyed. Unable to overthrow the Mighty One, he turned his sights on those that bore God's image. And we fell, and as Milton says, 'Our glory faded.' [6]

THE STORY OF ADAM AND EVE [7]

'And the Lord God formed a man's body from the dust of the ground and breathed into it the breath of life. And the man became a living person.' (Genesis 2:7)

From the beginning God is intimately involved with us. He doesn't form man from a distance -He gets His hands dirty making this model-man Adam. And then, when it comes time to bring him to life we read that God, 'breathed into his nostrils.'

17

Not particularly sterile, if you think about it, but very intimate. His breath of life causing the man to become alive.

Then to make Eve God plunged his hand into the blood and flesh of Adam's body to take a rib. God was fully involved physically in their creation.

All is good until we come to Genesis chapter 3 where we read how the first humans chose to rebel. As we'll see, Adam and Eve succumbed to the temptation of viewing God from a distorted perspective. Here in chapter 3 we are given many of the clues as to how such a beautiful world can become so damaged.

It begins with the first created woman, Eve, talking with the snake about the nature of the world, and God. Clearly the serpent is not there to be helpful but to engage in trickery and destruction. Being tricked always involves the subtle or blatant manipulation of fear, memory and shame. Eve, having never encountered anything but goodness, has no reason to doubt the snake so she assumes this is another good creature God has created.

Now the serpent was the shrewdest of all the creatures the Lord God had made.

> *'"Really", he asked the woman: "Did God REALLY say, You must not eat any of the fruit?" "Of course we may eat it," the woman told him, "it is only the fruit at the centre we are not allowed to eat. God says we must not eat it or even touch it or we will die." "You won't die," the serpent hissed. "God knows that your eyes will be opened when you eat it and you will become just like God, knowing everything, both good and evil."'* (Genesis 3:1-5)

With the first question the serpent evokes within the woman the dynamic of doubt, the first of a series of emotional shifts that occur within Eve. This first incident of human doubt was just the first link leading to calamity, yet we all have experienced it in one form or another. Doubt creates right-vs.-wrong thinking (Did I really say that? Did I measure that correctly? Does God love me? What if I'm wrong?). This doubt causes an undercurrent of distress, which leads to fear.

Often the most subtle expression of distress we experience has its roots in fear. This feeling of fear alerts us to danger and threat. For humans, threat is not limited to physical perils; we interpret danger not only in terms of our physicality but our emotions as well. We are aware of words and non-verbal messages, which can be hurtful, shaming and threatening, creating more fear. This fear often expresses itself in a form of doubt which is constantly at work within us and between us. We may fear when we doubt the love someone has declared for us; our adequacy as a parent; the ability of our boss to promote us; or even that there is a God who knows we are alive, let alone cares and provides for us or has affection for us. Doubt leading to fear is Eve's first distressing emotion.

In the opening sentence of Genesis 3, the serpent is often described as being 'crafty'. In other words, he's skilful in the art of trickery, and in order to trick Eve he first must lead her to doubt God's instruction. Notice his initial question to the woman in verse 1: '*Did God really say*,' *You must not eat from any tree of the garden*? As many have rightly observed, he's already misrepresenting history.

In Genesis 2 God tells Adam, '*You are free to eat from any tree in the garden but you must not eat from the tree of the knowledge of good and evil, for when you eat of it you will certainly die.*' (v16-17).

There is no indication of God being restrictive and ungenerous. These words indicate that He provided freedom to eat from any tree except one. Here we see the serpent creating doubt by challenging Eve's memory. Of course, God's prohibition was given to Adam before He created and brought the woman to the man (2:22). The man, therefore, may have been responsible for relaying this command to the woman. However, Eve replies by embellishing the command.

The woman said to the serpent, 'We may eat fruit from the trees in the garden, but God did say", "You must not eat fruit from the tree that is in the middle of the garden, and you must not touch it, or you will die."'
(Genesis 3:2-3)

When stressed, it is not unusual to remember accurately. We may exaggerate 'and you must not touch it' or omit bits of instruction in the heat of the moment. Of course this just further adds to our confusion and doubt. This was true for Eve and this confusion, doubt and fear with the desire to be like God and know everything, made the temptation to eat the apple irresistible.

 ' *That moment, their eyes were opened, and they suddenly felt shame at their nakedness. So they strung fig leaves together around their hips to cover themselves.*' (Genesis 3:7)

When we become self-conscious, rather than God-conscious, we try to defend ourselves and stop being open to each other. We then quickly see the faults and flaws in the other person in response to their own fear and shame.

Hans Anderson in his story, *'The Snow Queen'* reflects this aspect of the Devils trickery in our fall.

'An evil troll, actually the devil himself, makes a magic mirror that has the power to distort the appearance of things reflected in it. It fails to reflect all the good and beautiful aspects of people and things while it magnifies

22

all the bad and ugly aspects so that they look even worse than they really are. The devil teaches a devil school, and the devil and his pupils delight in taking the mirror throughout the world to distort everyone and everything. They enjoy how the mirror makes the loveliest landscapes look like boiled spinach. They then want to carry the mirror into heaven with the idea of making fools of the angels and God, but the higher they lift it, the more the mirror grins and shakes with delight. It shakes so much that it slips from their grasp and falls back to Earth where it shatters into billions of pieces - some no larger than a grain of sand. These splinters are blown around and get into people's hearts and eyes, making their hearts frozen like blocks of ice and their eyes like the troll mirror itself, only seeing the bad and ugly in people and things.'

Splinters in the eyes of our heart cause us to see the bad not the good, producing a form of blindness that stops us seeing God in this world. The following prayer is to cleanse you from this blindness.

PRAYER

In this chapter we looked at how the enemy causes us to have splinters in our eyes (*The Snow Queen*). The Bible speaks of this as being blinded by the 'god of this world' - Satan (2 Corinthians 4:4)

In the early church, when someone became a Christian, one of the first prayers was to administer release from this blindness, so that believers could see with the eyes and ears of their heart. Today many who are genuine believers need this cleansing of their hearts from the 'dust of this world' to enable them to see and hear clearly. We need to pray: -

Father God,

Thank you for the freedom Christ has won for me. Please continue to set me free from the enemy, he who would seek to deceive me, cause me to look away from You and has blinded my heart and minds.

Cleanse my heart and mind from his lies, I pray. Wash me clean where darkness has imprisoned me and please continue to cleanse me from the dust of this world. Amen

I believe Adam and Eve, realizing their nakedness, began to point at each other.

When we are covered in fear and shame, the differences we see between us and others are negative and accusatory rather than celebratory. We look at our differences with shock and feel embarrassed. However, after hiding from each other, Adam and Eve quickly move to the next inevitable step - they hide from God.

> `Toward evening they heard the Lord God walking about in the garden, so they hid themselves among the trees. The Lord God called to Adam, "Where are you"? He replied, "I heard you, so I hid. I was afraid because I was naked."'(Genesis 3:8-10)

One of the things we notice here is that God is walking towards them, coming to visit them in the cool of the evening breeze. God is everywhere, and we are never apart from God, and this must have been true in the Garden of Eden. The picture is of God walking towards them, so He could have been out of the picture to some degree. The nearest example I can think of is that of a mother with her baby. Whilst the mother is in the room she is aware of the baby but at special times she moves towards the baby to make more intimate contact.

Tozer explains it like this: -

'There is a difference between a presence and a manifest presence. It is a fine difference between a man's presence and his face. The same word and the same relative meaning, but not quite. If a man comes into the room and keeps his back turned to you, you can say, "He was in my presence for half an hour," or "I was in his presence for half an hour." But you do not have much fellowship with a man who keeps his back turned to you. It is when he turns his face to you that fellowship begins. There is a difference between God being present and God's face being manifest to his people.' [8]

God enjoys His relationship with Adam and Eve - He comes walking in the cool of the evening breeze to come and be with them. So God basically says 'What have you done'? 'Have you eaten the forbidden fruit'?

"'Yes", Adam admitted, "but it was the woman you gave me who brought me the fruit, and I ate it." Then the Lord God asked the woman, "How could you do such a thing"? "The serpent tricked me," she replied. "That's why I ate it." (Genesis 3:12-13)

Adam, when confronted by God, impulsively turns on Eve as a means of protecting himself. In his shame he blames her. He wants to deny his part in the encounter. He wants to deny his silence, complicity and passivity, as he stood by and watched Eve's conflict with the serpent. Eve then feels exposed and undefended so she follows Adam's leading and blames the serpent. Both avoid giving God a straight answer. When we are overwhelmed by fear and shame we too avoid giving a straight answer; we want to deny, cover-up, shame or blame someone else, rather than be truthful and then open the gift of confession and forgiveness.

God begins with a simple question, not in order to accuse (as the serpent had done) but to truly engage the couple. God is looking for an honest answer but Adam and Eve acting out of the fear and doubt produced by the serpent, avoid giving a straight answer.

They shy away from 'owning up' and confessing. We are often the same, feeling overwhelmed by our fear and shame and not wanting to experience any more painful feelings, we start to cover up. We are quick to explain that it is not our fault. We blame someone else or circumstances for our marriage that is in trouble, our conflict with the church leaders or the truth that we have succumbed to our addiction again. Adam could have answered 'Yes'. From Eve the response 'I ate some and gave it to him' would suffice.

At any time throughout their encounter with the serpent, Adam and Eve could have called out to God, asked Him what He thought about what the serpent was saying and remained connected in their relationship with God. Instead they listened to the serpent and allowed his instructions to worm their way into their thinking patterns and direct their actions. After that, of course, they felt an acute need to hide.

Hiding from God always causes us to feel more alone and isolated, but God doesn't leave them alone and comes calling to them. He comes asking 'Where are you'?, which I will write more about in chapter 3.

At no time during their encounter did Eve check with Adam, asking 'What did God say?' Nor did Eve ask God to explain to her why she is beginning to get this bad feeling of fear and shame. God has always made all of us with the capacity to choose, but in the face of fear Eve moved away from God and began to doubt his goodness, and then began to doubt herself, believing herself to be inadequate. This is how we behave, having doubted ourselves we try to fix ourselves before returning to God.

By allowing her doubts to override her trust in God, Eve in effect chooses knowledge over life, object over relationship. No longer experiencing the gift of the perfect relationship with God she loses the capacity to feel connected and secure. She is then forever working hard, striving to believe she is good enough.

She loses the gift of abundance and joy in being known by the One who is Love.

The serpent is always coaxing her further away from God because Satan's intention is always to move us further away, not towards God. At no point does he say, 'Oh I can see you're upset, and what I'm telling you must make you feel really uncomfortable and disorientated. Let's go and speak to God about this, I'm sure He can make you feel better.'

The early part of Genesis 3 is the complete opposite of Genesis 2. In Genesis 2:25 we read that '*the man and his wife were both naked and felt no shame.*' And now, one chapter later, the woman is no longer in a place of protective harmonious community but in a place of fear, shame, guilt and painful isolation.

Doubt, having weakened the trust relationship with God - she has the need to medicate the negative feelings by finding something she can control. She looks for - in Curt Thompson's language - a 'non-relational coping mechanism' [9] and chooses a piece of fruit.

We are often left in that state because we fail to trust God and do not fully understand what Jesus has done for us.

We also read in Genesis 1:1 '*The Spirit hovered [fluttered] over the face of the waters. For emphasis the rabbis translated the passage to 'the spirit of God fluttered above the face of the waters, like a dove.'* In the sacred writings of Judaism there is only one place where the spirit of God is likened to a dove and that is Genesis 1:1. [10] The next time there is a link between the Holy Spirit and the dove is at Jesus' baptism.

> '*At that time Jesus came from Nazareth in Galilee and was baptized by John in the Jordan. Just as Jesus was coming up out of the water, he saw heaven being torn open and the Spirit descending on him like a dove. And a voice came from heaven: "You are my Son, whom I love; with you I am well pleased."*' (Mark 1:9-11 NIV)

Familiarity has veiled some of the aspects of Jesus baptism. The picture of the dove is not particularly striking to us but the Jewish spectators would have made a very clear link between the presence of the dove and creation. Mark is purposefully

31

pointing back to the beginning of history - just as the creation was the project of a triune God, so now we see the Trinity again, in full view together - Jesus in bodily form, the Holy Spirit as a dove, and the voice of the Father.

According to the Bible, the Father, Son and Spirit glorify one another. Each person glorifies the other. The ancient fathers called this the dance of the Trinity.

C.S. Lewis writes, 'God is not a static being but a dynamic, pulsating activity, and life almost a kind of drama. Almost, if you will not think me irreverent, a kind of "dance."' [11]

Jesus' baptism is a new creation, a new beginning, a new invitation to come out of hiding and join the dance to celebrate.

The parallels continue. God speaks the world into being, humanity is created and the next thing that happens is a battle. Satan tempts the first human beings in the Garden of Eden, and they fall.

Jesus is baptized, the Father has covered him in words of affirmation and love, and the third person of the Trinity, the Holy Spirit, leads him into the wilderness.

> `Jesus, full of the Holy Spirit, left the Jordan and was led by the Spirit into the wilderness, where for forty days he was tempted by the devil. He ate nothing during those days, and at the end of them he was hungry.` (Luke 4:1-2 NIV)

He is led into battle, into temptation.

To Adam God said, 'Obey me about the tree and you will live.'

Jesus is tempted to be the centre of attention, have everyone admire Him and protect Himself, in order to stop glorifying the Father and step outside the dance. Jesus defeats Satan but the assaults continue until the climax takes place in another garden, the Garden of Gethsemane. There God said to Jesus 'Obey me about the tree' (only this time the tree was a cross) 'and you will die.' [12]

Jesus died that we may be born again, adopted back into our original family and reconnected to our blueprint, our ' who we are meant to be' identity. But this identity is marred, wounded, broken and so, although we have the potential to be sinless and eternal, we continue to fall short. We are works in progress – yet - because of ' *Christ in me the Hope of Glory* (Colossians 1:27) as we walk with Christ we learn to reveal more and more of our original nature, more of the person God created us to be.

> `*And we all, who with unveiled faces contemplate the Lord's glory, are being transformed into his image with ever-increasing glory, which comes from the Lord, who is the Spirit.*' (2 Corinthians 3:18 NIV)

We become more known in our original glory by unwrapping the great gifts of the Christian church, confession and forgiveness. I have used the word 'unwrap' because there are barriers to receiving these gifts, some of which we will explore in the next three chapters.

PRAYER

Father God, I pray that as I recognize more of my fear, shame, hiding and sinful responses to life, you would prompt me to not look inward in despair, or listen to condemning negative self talk. Help me always to lift my eyes and ears to you.

Help me to turn to you Lord Jesus acknowledging and confessing my sins.

I pray that I will begin to move toward you to stay ' in the dance' regardless of my sin - circumstances knowing that nothing can separate me from your love. Amen

2

The two great gifts given to the Christian Church are confession and forgiveness. These gifts are often obscured by a liturgy that has become faithless formality or, in response to this, neglected on account of a decision of no liturgy. Both extremes cause us to forget and not understand how to apply the foundations of our faith. The purpose of theology, teaching and liturgy is to make it possible for the gospel to be heard and understood in every generation.

So what are some of the difficulties for our contemporary culture to hear and understand? I think one of these is the false belief that to own up to anything or acknowledge wrongdoing in any way will make us feel worse. Within the Church we have often taken the diminished sin to a narrow view that sin is an offence against a divinely instituted law and we ourselves are bad because we break the law. As soon as we think or feel like this we have become enmeshed in a sin/shame struggle.

Of course, breaking the law is part of a biblical understanding of sin. The fact is the Bible's view of sin is much more complex. This will become evident throughout the book as we explore other aspects of sin such as, '*Falling short of the glory of God'* (Romans 3:23) which leads us to miss the target and not become all God intends us to be. Mark Biddle, an Old Testament theologian, notes that:

'The "sin as crime" metaphor ... addresses certain aspects of the problem of human existence. Yet although dominant in the Western popular mind, it does not fully reflect the biblical witness, nor provide a sufficient basis for the Church's ministry in addressing human wrongdoing and its consequences, nor take account of the insights of contemporary theological movements, philosophies and social sciences that do not confirm its validity as a thorough description of the problem of being human'. [13]

So many of us do not feel we are utterly depraved, evil and totally rebellious, yet somehow we don't feel good enough for God. The gift of confession is our passport into an intimate

37

relationship with God but our shame blocks us from entry. Shame is not an easy concept to define, it manifests in a variety of faces. Unfortunately, in the English language the word 'shame' is used for both good (appropriate) shame and bad/toxic (inappropriate) shame.

Healthy Shame

Good/appropriate shame alerts us to our sin; our separation from God and others. It is an awareness of our fallenness, a reminder of all we lost in the Garden of Eden. It nudges us to acknowledge the potential within us to sin, to control or hurt others, to hide, or fail to be an authentic human being. Healthy shame draws us towards our need of God and to receiving forgiveness. Good shame leads to life, to an intimate relationship with God.

Continual sin can silence the voice of healthy shame, as we read in Jeremiah 3:1-5. Here the prophet is using words relating to marital unfaithfulness to describe the sin of his people.

`If a man divorces a woman and she marries someone else, he is not to take her back again, for that would surely corrupt the land. But you have prostituted yourself with many lovers, says the Lord. Yet I am still calling you to come back to me.*

Look all around you. Is there anywhere in the entire land where you have not been defiled by your adulteries? You sit like a prostitute beside the road waiting for a client. You sit alone like a nomad in the desert. You have polluted the land with your prostitution and wickedness. That is why even the spring rains have failed. For you are a prostitute and are completely unashamed. Yet you say to me, 'Father, you have been my guide since the days of my youth. Surely you won't be angry about such a little thing! Surely you can forget it!' So you talk, and keep right on doing all the evil you can.'

Jeremiah depicts the relationship between Israel and God as a husband and wife in a marriage. More than mere intellectual assent is involved here; there is passion, a word which comes from the Latin word for suffering. God is passionate about our relationship with Him. He suffers when the covenant relationship is broken and Israel is unfaithful. So instead of stubbornly clinging to everything wrong, attempting to hide our sin or minimise it both to ourselves and to God, we need to confess. Nothing can separate us from the love of God. God is still calling us, but our insistence on sin deafens His voice to us.

TOXIC SHAME

The paradox is that inappropriate/bad, also known as toxic shame has the same effect. Sin can silence the voice of healthy shame, causing us to believe the lie that what we are doing isn't that bad so we have no need of God. Toxic shame also attempts to stop us confessing by causing us to hide from God, in the same way as Adam and Eve did. The prodigal son allows shame to convince him that he is disqualified from a relationship with his father - *'I am no longer worthy to be called your son'* (Luke 15:19). He returns to his father but expects to be defined by his past sin. He has no expectation of being cleansed, reconciled and loved. You can also hear the toxic shame in Peter's voice when he realises who Jesus really is, *'Go away from me, Lord; I am a sinful man!'* (Luke 5:8). Contrast this with Peter in John 21. When John says to Peter, *'It is the Lord!'* Peter immediately dresses (he was stripped to the waist), jumps into the water and swims ashore. Peter rushes towards Jesus despite having denied Him three times. This is the key to being free from toxic shame - whilst still aware of our fallenness and sin we go towards Jesus.

'Look! Here I stand at the door and knock.   If you hear me calling and open the door, I will come in, and we will share a meal as friends.' (Revelation 3:20)

This verse is written to Christians. Jesus is knocking on the doors of our heart. In verse 19 Jesus says *'I reprove and discipline those I love. Be earnest, therefore, and repent.'* Confession, repentance and asking for healing opens the door. Denial and defensiveness keeps the door closed. Jesus says 'Anyone who truly loves me will keep my word and my Father will love him and we shall come in and make our home in him.' We are God's home, yet so often we try and bar him from certain rooms; those rooms filled with unhealed hurts, unconfessed sins, painful or humiliating memories. Yet all the time Jesus is saying, I am here as a friend, let's look at this, let's sort it out - 'Come and sit and eat with me, come and sit and drink with me - let me love you.' The great sadness is that God already knows what is in the hidden rooms, and no matter what is there, still loves us. Christ wants to dwell in those deep shameful places and set up table but we do are afraid to join Him there - we want everything clean and tidy and nice before we will enter, whereas Christ enters these places in order to transform them.

Symptoms

'Shame is both described as a staining, defiling dis-ease rendering the sufferer worthless in his or her own sight.' [14]

It is also known as 'Inner torment, a sickness of the soul that divides us from self, others and God' [15]. As well as making us hide, it silences us, causes us to lie and to be self-reliant. It prevents us from receiving grace and truth where we need them the most.

Quoting Andy Comiskey: 'Shame is the raincoat of the soul repelling the living water that would otherwise establish us as the beloved of God.' [16] This shame 'raincoat' causes us to believe we are unworthy of love and honour. It can be an emotion of inferiority; forever 'less than'. We turn in against ourselves, hiding, unable to receive mercy, love or affirmation. Shame bars us from receiving life. It is a self-imposed exile, always on the outside, fearful of being known and therefore unable to be honest and self-revealing. We live diminished lives, believing the lie that we are bad people because we do bad things.

In severe cases it is like believing we are a leper on the inside, disfigured, hideous, causing others ('if only they really knew us') to be repelled. This leads us into an isolating self-hatred, which can descend into believing that we must remain solitary because this internalised pollutant can contaminate others. One man remained on the back row at several conferences for fear that his 'evil' would stain the team. Another lady could not take communion until last because she thought others might 'catch' something bad from her.

Shame can flood the whole self with acute, dreadful feelings of inadequacy, humiliation and the desire to be invisible. There is an inability to make eye contact (what if someone could look into our eyes and see our stained soul?!) The fear of exposure keeps us silent. We always desire some sort of cover when we feel exposed, vulnerable and embarrassed. We cover our faces with our hands or avert our gaze, pulling down the blinds on the windows to our soul. We 'put on a brave face' or speak of 'hoping the ground would open up and swallow me'.

Summing up the symptoms Gershen Kaufman writes:

> 'Shame is a strong sense of being uniquely and hopelessly different and less than other human beings. When you experience shame you feel isolated and alienated from others. It is as if you are standing alone on one side of a broken bridge while everyone else in the world stares at you from the other side.'[17]

The lies we believe imprison us. Toxic shame whispers to us, 'I am worthless, not eligible, not worthy to be a child of God; I am unclean, too dirty, too damaged, stained, polluted on the inside. I will contaminate others. I am not good enough, don't measure up, can't achieve anything, not holy enough. No-one would want to know me if they knew what I was really like.'

CONSEQUENCES OF SHAME

HIDING AND LYING

As I have already said, shame makes us hide and lie. When I first became a Christian, although I appeared very free in worship, I knew that on the inside I was holding back, locked inside myself. I went to a friend for prayer and the story of the woman with her alabaster jar came to her mind quite strongly.

`One of the Pharisees asked Jesus to come to his home for a meal, so Jesus accepted the invitation and sat down to eat. A certain immoral woman heard he was there and brought a beautiful (alabaster) jar filled with expensive perfume. Then she knelt behind him at his feet, weeping. Her tears fell on his feet, and she wiped them off* *with her hair. Then she kept kissing his feet and putting*

perfume on them.' (Luke 7: 36-38)

I found any thought of being like her totally unthinkable. I could see that she obviously loved Jesus very much, as I did, and was willing to sacrifice her security, her expensive perfume. But she was willing to do it publicly, causing embarrassment and negative attention. My shame meant I could not risk being noticed and, anyway, it would not occur to me to go close to Jesus. I would just look from the back of the crowd. Secondly, I felt the alabaster box was inside me and contained something horrible, probably a demon. Shortly after this I read a C S Lewis quote:

'It is nice to be still under the care of St Mary Magdalen ....The allegorical sense of her great action dawned on me the other day. The precious alabaster box which one must break over the Holy Feet is one's heart. Easier said than done. And the contents become perfume only when it is broken. While they are safe inside they are more like sewage. All very alarming.' [18]

'Alarming' being an understatement!

About this time a friend rang to say she had met this amazing Spirit-filled man - a prophet, who could look right into you and have amazing 'words of knowledge' - would Ron my husband and I like to go to dinner and meet him the following Friday? I could not think of anything worse!! So, I lied and said we had a previous engagement. In doing so I hid and closed the door on the potential for release and healing.

God, however, is amazingly kind, merciful and always desiring the best for us. Later that summer I was at a Don Double conference. The talk had been on 'Freedom in Worship'. I went forward for a general prayer. When I returned to my seat Michael Harper stood up and said, 'I have this word from the Lord which doesn't really fit in with what we are teaching on, but the Lord is saying there is someone here who feels they have a box inside them and they are frightened to open it because they believe it contains a demon. God is saying this is not true - it is full of all the criticism and hurts you have internalised over the years. Let the Holy Spirit come and break the box.' I began to cry and could not stop. A teenage boy next to me took his dirty hanky out of his jeans and gave it to me. His kindness made me cry more. I cried for about four hours: glorious, healing tears.

Even having wounds or internalised pain had until this time felt shameful. Everything had to be hidden. At this point God reminded me how in Arthurian times, knights would remove their armour and shirt to show their battle wounds. These scars were badges of honour. It began to occur to me that maybe everything was not my fault.

FALSE GUILT

Another aspect of shame is false guilt, which along with the internal lack of freedom to worship I also suffered with. Many people live with the continuous feeling of having done something wrong, or having not done enough. This is often linked with false responsibility. I felt like this, although I would not have recognized it as shame. As an antidote to this feeling, I decided that when I was in the house alone, every time I walked up and down the stairs I would declare myself 'not guilty'. So each time I would speak out loud 'I am not guilty, I declare myself not guilty in Jesus' Name', God, of course, didn't need to hear this declaration. I was merely agreeing with His word. I was the one who needed to hear and know! All of my mind, my heart and my soul needed to hear and receive God's verdict.

My false responsibility was the consequence of having a very sick, poorly sister. She suffered from very bad asthma. As a family it was understood that certain emotional issues could trigger an attack: if my sister became angry or too excited this could cause the asthma. So I, as a little girl, took on the responsibility of trying to keep everything OK. This was not anything my parents put on me; it was that I obviously wanted her well (for partly selfish reasons) so that the illness wouldn't affect outings and holidays. When she became unwell I felt guilty that I had failed, that I hadn't done enough to keep everything on an even keel. I was also angry that she was ill, though I internalised this since that felt very wicked because my sister was the sick one. I also felt sorry for myself *(why should I have a sister who is always ill!?)* but this made me feel even more guilty because I was the fortunate one. I never acknowledged that mixture of feelings until I received healing prayer and realized it also contained aspects of 'survivor's guilt.'

Children raised in the same home as a handicapped sibling feel as though they are living with someone who needs 90% of the attention. They often wish that they were handicapped, not only to gain some of the attention, but because they feel guilty for not being handicapped, for being well and for surviving. They have ambivalent feelings of compassion and anger about the intense feelings of anxiety generated by the situation, yet feel helpless to do anything about it. Nothing works to make the person better - it seems like a '*Catch 22*' situation with no-one the winner.

If we are healthier at any level than the other people in our family we can feel false guilt for being healthy. This is often known as 'survivor's guilt.' Surveys after the last World War found survivors of the concentration camps felt guilty. This can also be true for survivors of road accidents, national disasters or many similar situations. It was discovered that these feelings of guilt were not connected to any act or sin but existed merely because the person had been fortunate enough to survive.

The term was first used and identified during the 1960's. Several therapists recognized similar, if not identical conditions among holocaust survivors. In the 1980 film 'Ordinary People', Conrad Jarrett is a young man who struggles with surviving a sailing accident which killed his older brother. His false belief/guilt was, 'Maybe I was too selfish about saving myself.' Slowly Conrad realises that he is angry with his brother's recklessness and begins to accept his survival had nothing to do with his brother's death. Instead of expressing anger outwardly the survivor turns it in on himself. False guilt can often be embodiment of anger directed towards oneself.

CHILDHOOD SHAME

For some, the roots of toxic shame go deep. They can be attached to early abuse or abandonment, or to a life-long struggle with addiction, and can be either for ourselves or for our family. Some shame roots are generational where there have been centuries of cultural or ethnic shame.

Children can realize very early in life that there are real ethnic, economical and social differences.

Children become acutely aware of different dress codes, peer group pressure and the shaming experience of not being one of the 'in-crowd.' Parents may also have unrealistic expectations of a child and shame their child for not fulfilling them. This is particularly true in Asian families where to 'lose face' is the most humiliating of experiences. Children are controlled by sayings such as 'Shame on you!' or 'Don't bring shame on the family.' Poor parenting will also use shaming labels to discipline a child. Instead of explaining, 'What you did was naughty, selfish and spiteful,' poor parenting says 'You are naughty,' 'You are selfish,' and 'You are spiteful.' We can feel shame as adults when we have not been understood as children. One young lady, Susan, who came to see me for prayer, felt great shame because she was different from the rest of the family. Her parents, brother and sister were all sociable, outgoing, easygoing and sporty. Susan was an introvert and more anxious. She was not convinced that it would all 'be alright' as her mother told her. She was further confused by the fact that her mother was very emotionally intelligent when it came to reading her father's emotions. He ran a large company and Susan's mother was always able to anticipate any tiredness or worries he experienced. However, she really didn't understand Susan, which left Susan believing it was her fault and that there was 'something weird' about her. This caused her to feel falsely guilty. She could not connect and communicate with Mummy and felt deeply shamed.

As children we cannot assess parental expectations and recognize them as unrealistic - the subsequent failure therefore leads us to feel the shame of believing we are hopeless or stupid. We also believe we deserve the bad treatment we receive, whether it is the withholding of affirmation and attention, or abuse. Parents have the power to plant seeds of toxic shame in a child, and the more inadequate the parenting the deeper the sense of shame.

Children also suffer from believing the magic formulae that good things happen to good people and bad things happen to bad people. Therefore, if something bad happens, such as divorce, having an alcoholic parent or suffering abuse, the belief is this is happening 'because I am bad,' or 'I was not good enough to prevent this.' Children can think, 'I caused mummy's depression' or 'Daddy's bad temper' is my fault.

Social workers dealing with children from abusive homes have observed:

> 'The refusal of these children to characterize their parents as bad and by the intensity of their devotion to mothers and fathers who were both neglectful and abusive ... Children who would not accuse the worst parents of bad behaviour would easily accuse themselves of being bad children.' [19]

The truth is that children are totally powerless, and therefore feel safer being the bad ones rather than facing the terror that their behaviour cannot change a bad parent or situation. This continues into adulthood, where we find it easier to declare ourselves the guilty one regardless of the truth, because then maybe we have the power to change something or someone.

I used to find great false comfort and relief if I could rework a disagreement in my mind to conclude that I was guilty. It gave me an illusory sense of power: 'Maybe now I could rectify the situation or "fix it."'

Alice Miller speaks clearly of the trap for children of abusive parents.

> 'The abused inmates of a concentration camp ... are inwardly free to hate their persecutors. The opportunity to experience their feelings -even to share them with other inmates, prevented them from having to surrender their self... This opportunity does not exist for children. They must not hate their father, they cannot hate him ... They fear losing his love as a result. Thus children, unlike concentration camp inmates, are confronted by a tormentor they love.'[20]

We also carry into adult life the shaming of the family - even if only by association. If we had parents who were disruptive and socially unacceptable because of mental illness or alcoholism, we experienced the stares, ostracism or disapproval that was focused on them. One of the complexities of shame is that something we neither initiated nor desired may still leave us feeling the shame.

As mentioned earlier, some parenting is shaming through ignorance, but some can be intentional, i.e. shaming in order to punish or control. One lady from a very strict school appeared to be more damaged by the shaming tactics of her teacher than by the physical punishment she endured. When we asked the Holy Spirit to surface a memory from childhood to help her to be free from her fears, this is the memory that surfaced. Because she was fearful of the teachers she was a very good girl. She was just sitting at her desk not thinking anything when the teacher, with '32 eyes' following her, stood in front of Laura and said accusingly, 'I know what you are thinking; I know what you have done.' Completely innocent, yet completely shamed.

This same lady, a few years previously, had struggled with any concept of confession being a joyful gift. On that occasion she had the memory of her twelfth birthday party which her sister, Reona, had organized. Mother was away a lot so Reona (only two years older) was virtually the mother. Laura remembered in prayer how, at the party, she was told she was naughty -although she didn't know what she had done - and was made, in front of her 26 birthday guests, to kneel before Reona and say she was sorry - another shaming experience.

ETHNIC SHAME

The Message - John 4 - The Woman at the Well

'A woman, a Samaritan, came to draw water. Jesus said, "Would you give me a drink of water"? (His disciples had gone to the village to buy food for lunch.) The Samaritan woman, taken aback, asked, "How come you, a Jew, are asking me, a Samaritan woman, for a drink"? (Jews in those days wouldn't be caught dead talking to Samaritans.)

Jesus answered, "If you knew the generosity of God and who I am, you would be asking me for a drink, and I would give you fresh, living water." The woman said, "Sir, you don't even have a bucket to draw with, and this well is deep. So how are you going to get this 'living water'? Are you a better man than our ancestor Jacob, who dug this well and drank from it, he and his sons and livestock, and passed it down to us'"? Jesus said, "Everyone who drinks this water will get thirsty again and again. Anyone who drinks the water I give will never thirst—not ever. The water I give will be an artesian spring within, gushing fountains of endless life." The woman said, "Sir, give me this water so I won't ever get thirsty, won't ever have to come back to this well again!" He said, "Go call your husband and then come back." "I have no husband," she said.

"That's nicely put: I have no husband.' You've had five husbands, and the man you're living with now isn't even your husband. You spoke the truth there, sure enough."'

The woman at the well was not an innocent woman. In fact she knew she was guilty of sin, but her shame was not only linked to her lifestyle choices. She also suffered from ethnic shame. This type of shame can bar us from believing that we are candidates for God's love. She is expressing this awareness of the shame barrier when she asks Jesus why a Jew like himself would talk to a Samaritan woman. No respectable Jewish man would be seen talking to a Samaritan woman in public. She was a member of the hated mixed race who were rejected due to their ancestry, a joining of Gentile and Jewish blood. The Israelite forefathers had forsaken their spiritual and sexual laws by marrying foreigners.

The Samaritans were scorned, humiliated and made outcasts not for their sin but for the shameful inheritance of their race. The behaviour of the Jews would have continually made her feel inferior, of a lesser rank.

Gershen Kaufman says, 'People who belong to different cultural and racial groups, and who feel outcast or inferior because of it, live lives of unrelenting exposure to shame ... Whenever a group of individuals feel persecuted, disenfranchised, or looked down upon, their resulting shame and powerlessness inevitably become fused.' [21]

A lovely black lady, Doreen, used to come to see me to be healed from the wounds of childhood sexual abuse. As with so many people who suffer deep wounds of this nature, she was wrapped in layers of shame. She believed the lies that what had happened to her was her fault, she was somehow complicit and also, as an illegitimate child within a 'respectable' family she was blamed for existing. I often say in such circumstances after I have been praying for healing and release, 'Look at me, look in my eyes.' She had many reasons for shame but I did not expect her answer. '*I cannot look a white woman in the eyes*'- deep generational ethnic shame.

Apparently in some black cultures the 'lesser' does not make eye contact with the 'superior'. This can cause misunderstandings e.g. with white police officers who wrongly assume that an avoidance of eye contact is a sign of guilt.

CULTURAL SHAME

Western culture has a system of measuring that which is superior and that which is inferior, what is achievement and what is failure. We live with the pressure of trying to fit in and to receive accolades, awards or approval. We want to be considered worthy.

This desire for perfection can focus on our looks. Maybe our breasts aren't big enough, or are too big or our genitals not big enough. We are too skinny, not muscular enough or too fat. Of course, as children, these comparisons can lead to a daily ordeal of being bullied and shamed. Verbal abuse that is shaming is more deeply wounding than verbal abuse that is threatening. Shaming abuse leads to self-hatred, which leaves us feeling powerless. We often believe the lies, think we deserve what is being said and therefore don't want to tell anyone what is happening. Threatening abuse leads to fear, which maybe we can do something about, by enlisting help or avoiding the person or situation.

We can feel shame because we grew up poor, 'on the wrong side of the tracks.' Unless God heals these wounds, they remain lifelong scars. We can, as adults, maybe become better off financially than our friends yet still feel the pangs of cultural poverty shame. Maybe we speak with an accent which reveals our less acceptable background. We can feel cultural shame among 'posher' people.

These feelings of cultural shame can lead to self-hatred and a covering up of our past, with intense feelings of guilt and shame.

Brennan Manning writes: -

'The disparity between our ideal and real self, the grim spectre of past infidelities, the awareness that I'm not living what I believe, that I am not all that I ought to be, that I am not measuring up to others' expectations of demeanour and lifestyle, the relentless pressure of conformity, the midlife oppression of what I had hoped to become and what I have actually become, the obsession with personal dishonesty and self-centredness, and our mournful nostalgia for the Blue Lagoon, transform an expectant pilgrim people into a dispirited travelling troupe of brooding Hamlets, frightened Rullers and wiped-out Willie Lomans.

Alcoholism, workaholism, mounting addictive behaviours across the board and the alarming suicide rate indicate the magnitude of the problem.

In the struggle with self-hatred we obviously do not like what we see.   It is uncomfortable, if not intolerable, to confront our true selves and so, like runaway slaves, we either flee our own reality or manufacture a false self which is mostly admirable, mildly prepossessing and superficially happy.' [22]

Again, the shame/self-hatred stops us coming to God in healthy honesty with our confessions.

Being put in a shameful situation by circumstance or society as an adult can also affect us. Moira had been married for about 16 years. Her husband had been sick with a mixture of cancer and mental illness for about the last 8 years of their married life. She had two children and until the last six months of his life she had nursed him. During his last six months, whilst in hospital, he had met a nurse. He returned to the nurse's home to die and she arranged the funeral. Moira went to the funeral with her two children standing on the other side of the church and grave from the other mourners. I asked her how this made her feel and she said she felt so ashamed. She said she felt she had lost the respect of even being able to be the wife of the dead person and the mother of his children. We can see from this story, that there is nothing that she should be ashamed of. The sin was *against her,* yet the feelings of humiliation, of not being recognized as a wife and mother, of having 'lost respect', left her excluded and experiencing feelings of shame.

VICTIM SHAME

One of the main healings needed by someone who has survived sexual abuse, once they have understood that they were innocent not guilty, is healing from lingering shame. The severity of the abuse directly links to the depth of the shame.

One man in his late fifties said he had suffered the most incredible shame all of his life. This shame began when he was a baby. He was a very sickly child, unable to feed well. In fact his mother's milk poisoned him, which made her feel guilty and shamed, and baby absorbed these feelings. Then, through ill-

64

informed medical advice, he was left crying for long periods as he
had been put on a strict four-hourly feeding programme. This
left him, along with the separation anxiety, feeling that there
was something wrong with him, that no-one came because he
was unlovable - deep shame. [23] However, when we came to pray
about the shame a memory of sexual abuse surfaced, he was
made, by a cousin (at the age of 5 or 6) to watch teenagers
having sex. Because of his earlier life, he had no sense of being,
no inner core that could resist this. Nor, of course, could he worry
mummy. He had been 'enough trouble already.'

The picture I had was of someone very tiny with all the
windows and front door of his soul wide open so the full impact of
what had happened to him had flooded his whole being. He felt
shame because he knew he was involved in something wrong.
He needed prayer to understand that sin had been done *to him*.
He needed to be released from the sin against him and healed of
the shame.

'Fix our eyes on Jesus, the pioneer and perfecter of faith.
For the joy set before Him, He endured the cross, scorning its

65

shame and sat down at the right hand of the throne of God.'
(Hebrews 12:2)

Jesus scorns (despises, dismisses, disregards or looks with contempt as other translations put it) the shame. We need to do likewise – acknowledge and ask for healing from our wounds but not allow our feelings of shame to define us.

We need to be more aware of our shame in order to prevent ourselves from automatically turning to destructive coping mechanisms, as we may have done in the past. Remember our sinful response to shame is self-hatred. When we have been shamed we hate ourselves. We believe the shaming lies, the toxic whispers rather than the love words of our Heavenly Father.

Leanne Payne talks about shame being like a black disc sitting over the garden of our heart and blocking us the warmth (love) of God's sunshine and the rain of His (Holy Spirit). As mentioned earlier, Andy Comiskey speaks about shame being like a raincoat.

I see it like a magnetic cloak which attracts negative looks, words and thoughts and repels all loving words and acts of kindness.

(Please adapt the following prayers according to your story)

PRAYER FOR LIFTING THE CLOAK OF SHAME

"Father God, I come to you with the cloak of shame I have worn and laboured under all these years. I confess to you that I have believed a lie and put on this shame: the belief I was defective, not good enough, 'less than' and unable to change. I confess all the times I have believed I was a 'hopeless case' beyond transformation.

I have not lived in the truth that I was created by you, but have lived in the shame of the lie. I ask your forgiveness for believing these lies and being defined by my feelings of shame. I receive your forgiveness. Please come and cleanse me with the blood of Jesus and heal my wounds.

I reject, in the name of Jesus, all shaming words, looks and attitudes, and ask you to help me to replace them with your words of love. I choose to begin the process of forgiving those who have shamed me. I thank you Jesus that you died a shameful death, rejected, naked, outside the city wall.

I take off my cloak of shame and give it to you, Jesus, on the cross. I ask now Father that you will send your Holy Spirit to guide me as I work through the many areas of my life that have been affected. Bind truth to me I pray. Show me the areas where my behaviour needs to change and be with me as I find new ways of thinking and relating. Father, most of all I am sorry for hiding from you. Please help me always to turn towards you." [24] Amen

PRAYERS FOR INTERNALISED CHILDHOOD CULTURAL, ETHNIC FAMILY

ABUSE

'Do not be afraid; you will not be put to shame. Do not fear disgrace; you will not be humiliated. You will forget the shame of your youth and remember no more the reproach of your widowhood.

For your Maker is your husband—the LORD Almighty is his name—the Holy One of Israel is your Redeemer; he is called the God of all the earth. The LORD will call you back as if you were a wife deserted and distressed in spirit—a wife who married young, only to be rejected, says your God. Though the mountains be shaken and the hills be removed, yet my unfailing love for you will not be shaken nor my covenant of peace be removed, says the LORD, who has compassion on you.' (Isaiah 54:4-6, 10)

'Instead of your shame you will receive a double portion, and instead of disgrace you will rejoice in your inheritance. And so you will inherit a double portion in your land, and everlasting joy will be yours.' (Isaiah 61:7)

Father God, please help me where taking off my cloak is not enough because inside I believe the lie there is something wrong with me. I bring to you all the shaming words spoken to me or about me that I have swallowed. I bring to you my childhood memories of shame where I felt less than the other children because of poverty, education, race or class.

I ask you heal me where the shame was on the whole family because of alcoholism, mental illness or other behaviour considered socially inappropriate. I come before you with the pain these memories and thoughts evoke and ask you to cleanse and heal me.

I know that Satan is the father of lies and when I believe these lies I remain imprisoned in shame. Thank you that Jesus came to set the prisoners free. Thank you that the Holy Spirit leads us into all truth and truth sets us free. I ask that you will lead me into all truth – give me courage to believe you and start to experience freedom. Amen

PRAYER FOR GENERATIONAL SHAME

Father God, I come to you with the shame I have inherited. I can see the shame my mother/father wore – I know the family history of being outcasts, immigrants or never 'fitting in.' I am aware of the sins of illegitimacy, sexual immorality, gambling and illegal dealings that have brought shame on the family.

I now stand before you and confess the sins of my family and the ways they have allowed shame to be a barrier to life.

I ask now that you, Lord Jesus, and the power of you dying on the cross, come between me and previous generations. I ask you absorb into your body their sin and shame, and to release me from the effects. Heal my wounds – set me free.

And now Father, I ask that you will, through the cross of Jesus, bless to me all that is good in my inheritance and all the potential you intended for me. Amen

3

THE INVITATION

It doesn't interest me what you do for a living,

I want to know what you ache for,

And if you dare to dream of meeting your heart's longing.

It doesn't interest me how old you are,

I want to know if you will risk looking like a fool for love,

For your dream, for the adventure of being alive.

It doesn't interest me what planets are squaring your moon,

I want to know if you have touched the centre of your own

sorrow,

If you have been opened by life's betrayals,

Or have become shrivelled and closed from fear of further pain.

I want to know whether you can sit with pain, mine or your

own, without moving to hide it, or fade it, or fix it.

I want to know if you can be with joy, mine or your own; If you can

dance with wildness and let the ecstasy fill you to the tips of your

fingers and toes without cautioning us to be careful, to be

realistic, to remember the limitations of being human.

I want to know if you can be faithful,

And therefore trustworthy.

I want to know if you can see beauty,

Even when it is not pretty every day,

And if you can source your own life from its presence.

I want to know if you can live with failure, yours and mine,

And still stand on the edge of the lake

And shout to the silver of the full moon "Yes".

It doesn't interest me to know where you live

Or how much money you have.

I want to know if you can get up after the night of grief and despair,

Weary and bruised to the bone,

And do what needs to be done to feed the children.

It doesn't interest me who you know,

Or how you came to be here,

I want to know if you will stand in the centre of the fire with me

And not shrink back.

It doesn't interest me where or what or with whom you have studied,

I want to know what sustains you from the inside

When all else falls away.

I want to know if you can be alone with yourself,

And if you truly like the company you keep

In the empty moments. [25]

Oriah

The poem just read is calling us to a place of being known - however, we are like Adam and Eve. As we saw in Chapter 1, their response to sin was to hide from themselves, God and each other. We share similar feelings as Adam and Eve - the shame, guilt and fear - and we behave in the same way. We lie, blame and hide; we seek to protect ourselves by covering ourselves with 'fig leaves'. Adam and Eve experienced separation from God. They went from total freedom and security to fearful insecurity. They fell from God-consciousness into self-consciousness. As soon as God saw them hiding, He knew they had eaten the apple. Their behaviour was as strong as the evidence when a child denies eating a doughnut but with all the sugar and jam around his or her mouth.

Hiding is the first fundamental behavioural outcome of sin: It leads me to hide parts of myself from other parts of me, I hide from other people and I hide from God. Just like shame, this hiding blocks me from receiving God's forgiveness, grace and mercy. It stops me receiving the gift of confession.

God, however, doesn't want us covered with fig leaves, hidden in isolation. God did not come calling for Adam and Eve with an accusatory voice, saying *'I know what you have done.'* He asks *'Where are you'?* (Genesis 3: 9). He gives them the opportunity to reveal themselves. He does not expose, condemn or shame Adam and Eve but seeks them out, making the first move towards reconciliation, inviting them back 'home.' Adam responds *'I heard you and I was afraid because I was naked, so I hid.'* (Genesis 3:10).

As Curt Thompson[26] explains: -

'Adam and Eve's shame has doubled back on itself. Eve's fear led to shame, which led to hiding (fig leaves) - which led to fear, which led to shame and hiding (behind the trees). This is the basic pattern of sin. It begins with not paying attention - to the voice of the one who tells us we are loved beyond comprehension and who repeatedly asks us where we are.'

God will bring us out from behind the trees so we can address the fear, shame and strategies we employ to cover ourselves.

As we saw in Chapter 1, God asks questions hoping for an honest response. God asks *'Who told you that you were naked? Have you eaten from the tree that I commanded you not to eat from*? (Genesis 3: 11). Again, God does not initially focus on their eating of the forbidden fruit, but in essence says, 'What have you done to create those feelings of shame and self-consciousness that have caused you to hide'?

What would have happened if, at this point, they had run towards God to confess? Imagine if Adam had said, '"I am really sorry I ate the fruit. Eve and I were taken in by that snake. We should have listened to You. I should have said something but I didn't. I just kept quiet. I feel bad. Please forgive and heal me". Imagine if Eve had said "I am so sorry I gave the fruit to Adam. The snake tricked me into believing I needed more than You had provided. Please forgive me and heal these bad feelings I am experiencing.'"

We do not know what God's response would have been, or how different the world would have been, but we do know that following Jesus' death on the cross for our sin, we can come out of hiding and confess.

But so often, like Adam and Eve, we fail to do this and continue to wear our fig leaves. In psychology we speak about defence mechanism, survival aids, masks and false personae -the Bible speaks about fig leaves. I believe God has made us with the ability to devise defensive/survival techniques. This is how we survive abuse and destructive situations.

Our difficulties arise when we continue in this behaviour using our weapons of war when peace has come! Jesus promises us a peace which passes all understanding, but we continue to hide. There is a story of an American soldier found hiding in the jungle a long time after the Vietnamese war was over, fearful to come out and unaware that peace had come [27]. What are the jungles we hide in? What are some of our 'fig leaves'?

THE FIG LEAF OF PLAYING A ROLE

Patterns of behaviour in our family of origin can cause us to hide behind a fig leaf of playing a role. These stem from unhealthy family dynamics and were first identified by people working with alcoholics and written about in *Adult Children of Alcoholics (*Janet Geringer Woititz.*)* In unhealthy families there is no honest dialogue and very little reality. It is more important to give the right answer that doesn't 'rock the boat' than a truthful answer. You may have more than one role.

1. Problem person

Everyone revolves around them. This person may be a substance addict, rageaholic, workaholic or someone who is fragile and prone to depression. It can be a sick or special needs child. It is the person who always has to be considered, who takes priority, who is the focus of the family.

2. Lost Child

Someone who withdraws from conflict and/or anger and retreats into a fantasy world. He/she has an internal dialogue, is self-reliant and defends by detaching.

3. Hero

A 'caretaker'/rescuer who feels they've got to sort it out. 'Messiah'/'Saviour.' Their main mission in life is to make everyone happy by solving all the problems. This is also a form of hiding because there is no self-revealing.

4. Scapegoat

This person is blamed and takes the blame.   He or she takes on false responsibility   ('Everything is my fault').

5. Mascot

The family member who rescues with jokes and uses jokes or banter to avoid intimacy.

6. Surrogate husband

This is the role of 'Mummy's little prince' - having to look after mother. He may be her passport to a social life, protector against Daddy or her intimate confidante. Many boundaries are broken by this enforced playing of a role

7. Surrogate wife

The role of 'Daddy's little princess.' This role can involve anything from sexual abuse and cultivating a special relationship through to wanting a childlike princess kept in a gilded cage and continually indulged. In the news we have been made aware of cases of men keeping their daughters 'imprisoned', and even having children by them. It may be that Daddy cannot cope with a fully grown woman/wife so prefers time with his daughter. Again, complex boundaries are broken in these unhealthy relationships.

How does this hiding behind our roles play out in adult life? You may have already recognised some of your patterns of behaviour. I was either the lost child or the hero.

1. The Lost Child

As a child I would often withdraw into books or fantasy. Later, as an adult, I found I wanted to withdraw from difficult situations. One example of this was when I was in Denmark following a conference. A large team of us were standing on a small Danish station platform being very noisy and very untidy. We had lots of baggage and sound equipment, which had spread along the whole platform. I felt embarrassed by this and found myself at the far end of the platform with my back to everyone pretending to read a Danish railway timetable!! (A strong desire to distance myself and hide!)

2. The Hero

The hero (as I explained in Chapter 2 - I wanted to keep my sister well) always suffers from false responsibility and the subsequent anger or shame when they fail. Heroes often enter the caring professions and hide behind their role. There is very little self-revealing as most relationships are built around the need to care for or fix someone else. The fig leaf on the hero creates an unequal exchange relationship.

3. The Scapegoat

This person in adult life spends their time apologising. I worked in one particular group where one of the men, Mark, took responsibility for and apologised for everything that went wrong even though we all knew it wasn't his fault. Whenever we confronted this he apologised for apologising. This made it very difficult to have any real intimate conversation.

4. Mascot

Humour can be a very healing ingredient in relationships and, when healthy, helps us not take ourselves too seriously. However, it can be used as a fig leaf to defuse (avoid) any painful situation by making a joke. It means that unless someone recognises the tactic everyone backs off the difficult conversation and laughs. Continuous joke-telling and banter has the effect of denying any intimacy.

5. Surrogate Husband

This role play inhibits healthy relationships. One man, Alan, felt his job in life was to keep Mummy happy. As a result, in his adult relationships, any woman, even with legitimate needs, made him feel she was demanding of him, crowding him, tiring him and therefore making him feel selfish. He normally withdrew and sabotaged the relationship. Another man, Tony, had been

'Mummy's little prince.' She would take him shopping with her and he would admire all her new clothes and she would buy him a treat. After he was married he realised he wanted his wife to buy him treats and look after him and he withdrew feeling hard done by and self-pitying when this didn't happen.

6. Surrogate Wife

The extent of the boundary-breaking involved in this role obviously contributes to the damage and subsequent amount of hiding. This can be across the spectrum from extreme defensive detachment, whereby one hides in a fortress, through to hiding behind a fig leaf. (Extreme cases need more attention than I am giving here). For example, Anne's father adored her. She was clever, attractive and popular and her father felt no boy was good enough for her. When she did finally find her man he was also clever, handsome and popular. They were well-matched. However, Anne struggled to come to terms with her husband's inability to live up to Daddy. He didn't always indulge her, didn't worship her in her gilded cage but treated her like a flesh-and-blood woman. She withdrew hurt and confused. Daddy confirmed she was not being well treated so she hid behind the fig leaf of

the fragile princess.

GENERAL PRAYER FOR THE REMOVAL OF CURSE OF FIG LEAVES

Lord Jesus,

Thank you that your desire is for all my fig leaves to wither and die. I ask now that you will help me name my fig leaves. Release to me a gift of truth whereby I can clearly see all of my hiding tactics.

I now confess the fig leaves (name them) (It is very important that we name our fig leaves. This is not a passive 'lay down and let God' prayer, it is a 'coming out of hiding and taking responsibility' prayer) as sin and ask for Your forgiveness. I ask now that You will remove - in whatever way You wish - these coverings. Please allow me, with the 'eyes and ears of my heart'; to receive Your forgiveness and to see the fig leaves go.

And now, Father, I ask for new clothes, those I need to reflect Your glory and be able to stand authentically as Your royal son/daughter. Thank you that we are given bright clean shining pure linen to wear. Amen.

HIDING IN MARRAIGE

Hiding leaves us lonely, even in our marriages. John and Stasi Eldridge talk about this.

John: 'As a man, Adam was endowed with the image of God primarily in his strength - a strength given him for the benefit of others. It's not about big muscles, but about INNER strength. Notice that when men fail they tend to fail in one of two ways - either they become passive and silent, or they become domineering and violent. They either don't offer their strength or they wield it in harmful ways. I did both - I was utterly passive when it came to offering Stasi intimacy; I ran and hid at work. And I was practically violent in my driven perfectionism.'

Stasi: 'As a woman, God endowed Eve with beauty - an INNER beauty often expressed in tenderness and vulnerability. Notice that when women fail they tend to become either controlling or desperately needy. Either they refuse to offer vulnerability or they ask their man to fill the ache in their soul. I did both - my weight was a way of

84

controlling my world and insulating myself from intimacy.
My fear that I was a disappointment kept me from offering
my true self. And yet I would look to John to fill me.' [28]

THE FIG LEAF OF IMAGE

As Paul McCartney wrote in his song about lonely people:
'Eleanor Rigby ... waits at the window, wearing the face that she
keeps in a jar by the door. Who is it for'.....?

To achieve a healthy way of being we must pass from a self-
centred, adolescent stage, and experience healing from the effects
of living with families who are more focused on image and roles
than honesty.

Leanne Payne writes, 'Whoever does not accept himself is
engrossed with himself.'[29] The myth of Narcissus is the story of
adolescence. The youth, Narcissus, looks at his own reflection in
the water and falls in love with himself. With his attention fixed on
his own image, he tumbles into the water and drowns. This myth
is especially appropriate to the twenty-first century.

This need for image can be seen in society at large – in teenagers in particular – wearing labels on the outside – brand names, logos, telling the world we belong, we are okay, we've got the right image. However, many of us have not emerged out of the narcissistic adolescent stage that C .S Lewis calls 'the dark ages in every life' -that time when 'the most un-ideal senses and ambitions have been restlessly, even manically awake.' [30]

This excessive need to conform, and fearful self-consciousness, is part of adolescence but we are not meant to be stuck there or we become unrealistic images creating our own identity.

But the fact that a Christian has not accepted himself, indeed, has not entirely emerged out of the immature, narcissistic state, is not always so apparent. A Christian man, for example, unaffirmed as a man, may very well be fixed on an image of himself as a successful businessman, priest, financial wizard, whatever. Just like Narcissus, he has 'fallen into his own image' and the true self is drowned. Such a man does not know his identity as a person in Christ; indeed, he does not know his true identity. He is a masked man, one whose worth and identity are tied up in his role or roles. How he is perceived socially is more important to him than who he is privately. His roles obscure his failure to accept himself. We hide behind our image, more worried about what others, the neighbours may think, than what is actually taking place behind the closed doors we call home. This can be called 'external referencing.'

1 Samuel 16 :7 - '*The Lord does not look at the things man looks at. Man looks at the outward appearance but the Lord looks at the heart.*' I believe part of being holy is being transparent, authentic and having integrity.

When we are born again we become a new person inside. God's Holy Spirit comes and indwells us in union with our innermost being. We become a brand new creation. Do we get different colour hair? Or eyes? No, so what is made new? God begins to transform us from the inside out. When we don't understand this or trust in the process, we create a brand new person on the outside - we design ourselves, play a role.

PRAYER FOR THE REMOVAL OF THE FIG LEAF OF IMAGE

Father God, I confess the fig leaf of image. I confess I am overly concerned with the way I look, what image my home reflects, how I speak and many other aspects of trying to create an image/illusion that will help me be acceptable to those I want to belong with or want to impress. I acknowledge that it does not work – it merely leaves me feeling fraudulent and desirous to cover up even more.

Please forgive me and give me the courage to be the person you made me to be, nothing less and nothing more. Amen

FIG LEAF OF THE CHRISTIAN PERSONA

This fig leaf is a variety of different colours. Bob George calls it 'legalism':

'Imagine yourself in a large house in which are living both deaf and hearing people. They are all mixed together and you can't tell by looking who is deaf and who has hearing. Sitting in a room by himself is a man. As you watch you notice that he is tapping his toes rhythmically and snapping his fingers in time. You know what is happening. He's listening to music and obviously enjoying himself. His whole body wants to respond to what his ears are receiving. There's nothing strange or mysterious about it.

But now let's add a new person to the scene. One of the deaf persons opens the door and enters the room. He immediately sees the first man and walks over to him and smiles a greeting. The deaf man watches the music-lover for a few moments. 'He sure seems to be enjoying himself he thinks, "I think I'll try it too." So the deaf man sits next to the first man and begins to imitate him. Awkwardly and

89

haltingly at first he tries to snap his fingers, tap his toes, and move like the person next to him. Everybody has some sense of rhythm whether they can hear or not. After a little practice the deaf man is snapping and tapping in time with the first man. He even smiles a little and shrugs: "It's not that much" he thinks, "but it's okay."

Let's now add our final factor to the story. A third man walks into the room. What does he see? - Two men apparently doing the same thing. But is there a difference? Absolutely! All the difference in the world! The first man's actions are natural responses to the music he hears. The deaf man is only imitating those outward actions - even though he can't hear a noise. That is the difference between real Christianity and legalism'! [31]

Revelation 3 v 1: '*I know your reputation as a large and active church but you are dead*'! We learn the jargon. We learn what's culturally acceptable. We become obsessed with performance. We look at people with dramatic gifts rather than character, and can be deceived.

Whenever the children of Israel complained Moses turned to God for help. However, late in their journey Moses let his anger and frustration with the people erupt in disrespect towards God. Instead of speaking to the rock, as God had commanded, Moses struck it, as he had on a previous occasion, to bring forth water (Numbers 20: 8-11). Even though God viewed this disobedience with such severity that Moses was excluded from entering Canaan (Numbers 20:12 and Deuteronomy 32:51) the water still came out of the rock! Judging by the performance there was no indication of Moses' sin.

Gifts are not evidence of holiness. They are not merit awards, not 'GSCEs', but like wedding presents, a celebration of union. Both my daughters-in-law were bought food processors when they were married, not because at the time they could cook, but to bless the marriage and celebrate the union. We can be born again, moving in the gifts and being seen by others to be okay on the outside though we know we have a mess on the inside, that we are not who we are perceived to be.

We need to learn that we are 'becoming' people. I am not the person I was, nor am I the person I am going to be! Whether it's a shameful memory, a secret compulsion or an unhealed part of ourselves, we need to understand that the pathway to wholeness is being realistic, honest and vulnerable. We need to come out of hiding.

If we don't accept ourselves, instead of allowing God to change us from the inside out, we put on our Christian 'persona', learn the jargon and attend the meetings and the gap between our true self and our persona/image gets larger. We become like an enhanced CV or a touched up photograph.

Hebrews 4:13 says, *'Nothing in all creation is hidden from God's sight. Everything is uncovered and laid bare before the eyes of Him to whom we must give account.'*

PRAYER FOR THE REMOVAL OF THE FIG LEAF OF A CHRISTIAN

PERSONA

Father God, please forgive me where I have worked out what type of Christian appears mature and acceptable and have portrayed myself accordingly.

Forgive me where I am living behind my 'digitally enhanced photograph', where I am less than truthful with my Christian friends and where my spirituality is sometimes just my 'Sunday best'. Please strengthen me to deal with other people's pressures and reactions. Help me to choose authenticity over and above popularity.

Please forgive me and help me to come out of hiding and trust you to cover me in your love and affirmation as I seek real authentic relationships. Amen

FIG LEAF OF THE GOOD GIRL/ GOOD BOY

Jesus said 'woe' to the Pharisees because they made clean the outside of the cup but not the inside. Matthew 23:26 (ISV) says, '*You blind Pharisee! First clean the inside of the cup, so that its outside may also be clean.*' Jesus condemned the Pharisees because it was a foolish thing for a man to wash only the outside of a cup, which is to be only looked at, and leave the inside, which is to be used, dirty.

This is well illustrated in Zechariah 3. In the first verse Zechariah is transported into the centre of the Temple where he sees Joshua, the High Priest.

'*Then the angel showed me Joshua the high priest standing before the angel of the LORD. The Accuser, Satan, was there at the angel's right hand, making accusations against Joshua.*' (Zechariah 3:1)

'The temple had three parts: the outer court, the inner court, and the holy of holies. The holy of holies was completely surrounded by a thick veil. Inside was the Ark of the Covenant,

94

on top of it was the mercy seat, and the **shekinah** glory of God, the very presence and face of God, appeared over the mercy seat.

Only one person on one day of the year was allowed to go into the holy of holies: the high priest of Israel, on the Day of Atonement, also known as Yom Kippur. Zechariah, then, was experiencing a vision from the centre of the temple, inside the holy of holies, and he saw Joshua the high priest standing before the Lord on Yom Kippur.

An enormous amount of preparation took place for the Day of Atonement. A week beforehand, the high priest was put into seclusion—taken away from his home and into a place where he was completely alone. Why? So he wouldn't accidentally touch or eat anything unclean. Clean food was brought to him, and he'd wash his body and prepare his heart. The night before the Day of Atonement he didn't go to bed; he stayed up all night praying and reading God's Word to purify his soul. Then on Yom Kippur he bathed head to toe and dressed in pure, unstained white linen. Then he went into the holy of holies and offered an animal sacrifice to God to atone, or pay the penalty for, his own sins. After that he came out and bathed completely again, and new white linen was put on him, and he went in again, this time sacrificing for the sins of the priests. But that's not all. He would come out a third time, and he bathed again from head to toe and they dressed him in brand-new pure linen, and he went into the holy of holies and offered the sacrifice necessary to atone for the sins of all the people.

All this was done publicly. The temple was crowded, and those in attendance watched closely. There was a thin screen, which he bathed behind but the people were present: They saw him bathe, dress, go in and come back out. He was their representative before God, and they were there encouraging him. They were very concerned to make sure that everything was done properly and with purity because he represented them before God. When the high priest went before God there wasn't a speck on him; he was as pure as pure can be. Only if you understand that do you realise why the next lines of the prophesy in Zechariah 3 were so shocking: Zechariah saw Joshua the high priest standing before the presence of God in the holy of holies – but Joshua's garments were covered in excrement. He was absolutely defiled. Zechariah couldn't believe his eyes. How could that have happened? There's no way that the Israelites would ever have allowed the high priest to appear before God like that. God was giving Zechariah a prophetic vision so that he could see us the way that God sees us. In spite of all of our efforts to be pure, to be good, to be moral, to cleanse ourselves, God sees our hearts.'[32]

We are what we are inwardly. Outward motives may keep the outside clean but only if the heart and spirit are made new will there be a newness of life. Jesus says that we should cleanse first that which is within the cup so that the outside may be clean also. The greatest concern of all men should be inward purity, that their hearts be purified by faith in the blood of Christ.

So often, like the Pharisees, we present ourselves as more emotionally healthy than we really are, more morally upright. We present a 'good' false self, a Christian persona. This is a common response to shame and blocks us from receiving God's grace where we most need it. Unless we confess this - or in leadership recognise it - the real person remains untouched by the light of Christ. We remain cut off from God's love. We become compliant, fearful

that we are flawed and unlovable ('If you really knew me' ...).

Like a chameleon we 'change colour' according to the situation.

The Christian community often approves of the good false self but

this leads to self-deception since anything that belies the good

girl/boy image must be buried and denied. This means we often

put others first in the wrong way: the need for approval is more

important to us than moral or spiritual maturity.

PRAYER FOR THE REMOVAL OF THE FIG LEAF OF BEING THE

GOOD GIRL/BOY

Forgive me Father because I am forever striving and doing to please You and others. Forgive me where I try to make amends for the past by good works.

Thank you Father that you tell Joshua, the High Priest to 'take off his filthy clothes'. (Zechariah 3:4)

I take my good girl/boy clothes off. I confess I am often like the Pharisees wanting to appear good. Father, you say to Joshua, "I have taken away your sin; I will put rich garments on you." Thank you that through Jesus you have taken my sin and I can receive your rich garments. Amen

FIG LEAF OF THE SUPER-PERSON

The 'super-person' we think we ought to be can become an idol. We can devote much of our lives to making sure the right (powerful) people are pleased with us.

The more we pursue this hopeless task the less and less pleased we become with ourselves. We respond to their expectations and become dissatisfied with ourselves. We become split, hiding our true self whilst trying to fulfil/become the person we/others think we ought to be. This can involve a distorted image of God if we have an image of a demanding God we have to please.

We experience guilt and shame because we don't measure up to the perfect person we have in our head. We have some ideal in our heads that all the 'how to' books on looks, achieving, being spiritual etc, feeds. We internalise the messages that we must be the perfect daughter/son, husband/wife, mother/father, employer/employees, always able to witness or the perfect Christian, which means being a reliable church member with perfect, disciplined, reading of the Bible, praying, interceding, meditating, and giving ... we can't do it!! [33]

God doesn't define us by what we can't do, by what we are not and nor should we! We usually end up with a false sense of guilt and subsequent shame because we don't' function like a super-person - who isn't real anyway! Bob George calls this the 'phantom Christian':

'Often ... it's not even God's standards that they are trying to keep, but regulations imposed by themselves or other people. There is a certain mind-set that is especially destructive called the "Phantom Christian". The "Phantom Christian" is that imaginary person that many of us are continually comparing ourselves to. He is the super-spiritual man who gets up every day at 4.00 am so he can pray for four hours. Then he reads his Bible for four hours. He goes to work (at which he is tops in his field), where he effectively shares Christ with everyone in his office. He teaches several Bible studies, goes to church every time the doors are open and serves on several committees. He is also

101

a wonderful spiritual leader at home, a sterling example of a loving husband and father, who leads stimulating family devotions every day for his "Proverbs 31" wife and perfect children!

Of course no-one could live up to such a standard. Even if some person had the ability he would still need 100 hours in a day! Rationally we all know that the Phantom Christian is ridiculous, but the problem is that he is never brought to our consciousness. He is a vague ghost that sits in the back of our minds creating a sense of failure to measure up. That is the reason why many, many Christians live under continual guilt.

For those who believe that the Phantom Christian is God's standard for acceptance, God seems a million miles away, sitting in heaven with His arms folded in disapproval.   They don't bother offering prayers because they know He would never answer them.' [34]

This need for the approval of others, and a fear they may be doing better than us, can lead us into hiding in someone else's views, suggestion or armour.

PRAYER FOR THE REMOVAL OF THE FIG LEAF OF THE SUPER-

PERSON

Father God, I confess and smash the idol of the super-person. The 'phantom Christian' who mocks me with impossible demands. I am sorry I have listened and responded. Set me free I pray.

Thank you that your yoke is easy and your burden is light. Give me courage to be real. Give me courage to say no, both to others demands and the unreasonable expectations of my own unhealed voice. Amen.

Cast your deadly 'doing' down

Down at Jesus feet

Stand in Him, in Him alone

Gloriously complete. [35]

FIG LEAF OF FALSE ARMOUR

(1 Samuel 16). Rejected by his family, David isn't even sent for by Jesse when Samuel arrives. Samuel asks: 'Have you any more sons?' Jesse's reply *is* 'Well, yes, there's the runt out with the sheep.' Samuel, however, anoints him. There is no indication that his brothers acknowledge this although, 'The Spirit of the Lord came mightily upon him.' Earlier Samuel had said, 'The Lord has not chosen any of these,' *so* although they would not have known David was being anointed as King they knew the Lord had chosen him.

Soon after this David is asked to serve at Saul's Court because he is a good musician. Saul liked David very much.' So now he spends his time between two situations: the fields with the sheep and a father who had overlooked him, and the palace with a harp and a king who likes him. Then Goliath arrives on the scene, and all of the army are terrified, deeply shaken and without hope. In 1 Samuel 17, David arrives with provisions and starts to ask questions about the giant and the reward. Again, his brother is nasty to him, accusing him of pride, dishonesty and wanting to see the battle. He puts him down saying, 'What about tending that scrawny flock of sheep'? Saul hears of David's questions and sends for him. After some discussion he offers David his armour to protect him and to help him because at this point he wants the best for David and he certainly wants victory.

Despite being unaffirmed by his family and probably recognising Saul has his welfare at heart David tries it on but has the sense to realise that it doesn't fit so David refuses to wear the armour. I think this is very brave. How often do we put on someone else's armour?

Maybe, like me, you come from a family that didn't understand you; you didn't fit in, you certainly weren't the favourite. Then you find someone or somewhere that likes you and appreciates your gifts - maybe it's a church, a friend, a partner - but you're still a little bit outside. Then the opportunity comes (Saul sends for David) - you are offered a job, ministry, or something, and then the armour - you are given advice by a person or group that you desperately want to fit in with! If it were me at this point, apart from wanting to please my 'Saul' whoever this is, I would be thinking 'Perhaps he/they know best? After all, he/they have won several battles - churches, campaigns, ministry, who am I? What do I know'? I think it is very easy to slip into someone else's armour.

Another thought would be 'After all, he sent for me. God has opened this door so I don't want to mess it up by refusing his well-intentioned offer.' The subtlety of this can be seen in how often we fit into the Church's way of speaking, teaching or even the clothes we wear.

PRAYER FOR THE REMOVAL OF THE FIG LEAF OF FALSE ARMOUR

Father God, please forgive me where I have not trusted the person you made me to be. Forgive me where I have done as others have said without checking with you.

Forgive me where I have always assumed that others are always right even to the extent of disobeying your inner voice to me. Forgive me where I have confused others good intent with your word.

I now take off this false armour and choose to trust you and your ways for my life. Amen

FIG LEAF OF DENYING OUR PAST

Another way we enhance our image is by recreating our past. So often the temptation to impress others causes us to either make our past more colourful and lurid than it really was or we exaggerate our achievements, such as our education results, past jobs or successes. The more we hide the more difficult we find it to open the gift of confession.

A successful musician, Michael, came for prayer with feelings of isolation, not fitting in and believing others in the church looked down on him and didn't take him seriously. He lived in suburbia, a stockbrokers' area. He was born in a small, northern mining town but because of his musical talent had won a scholarship to the local public school. When we prayed and asked God the root of some of his difficulties he remembered this incident:

One Saturday afternoon he was walking down the street with his friends from school when he saw his father standing outside the cinema where he was the commissionaire. Embarrassed, as his friends' fathers were doctors or solicitors etc,

109

Michael dived into Woolworths taking his friends with him. When he came out his father was nowhere to be seen - he had gone into the foyer, but Michael knew his Dad had seen him. They never spoke of it. When I asked 'And how do you tell your story now'? He replied, 'Oh I just name the school I went to.'

He is not the same person he would have been if he had not won a scholarship but the person he now is could include his first eleven years. He didn't need to hide, but he continued to feel all the 'non-belonging' he experienced at school plus the guilt of his survival tactics as he continued to live behind his fig leaf of denying his past with the subsequent shame and pretending.

We can also deny our past by making it more sinful or more glamorous than the truth. One man, Stuart, came to see me having been sent by his church because of relationship difficulties. He was quite well-known as a speaker at evangelistic meetings, as he said his conversion was after a life of crime and of being in prison for GBH. Unfortunately, the more he stuck to this story, the gap between how he presented and his internal struggles increased. He returned to using drugs and then to stealing.

It was years later that I learned he had been in prison because he was a rent boy, so the shame that had caused him to wrap himself in a new story blocked him receiving God's transforming, healing love.

The other danger is to rely too much on our past.

PRAYER FOR REMOVING THE FIG LEAF OF DENYING THE PAST

Father, I come to you with my re-created past. I am sorry where I have deliberately lied. Please forgive me where I have told 'my' story so many times and deceived myself so that I no longer know the truth. Help me to tell my story without making it 'better' than it was but also without seeing myself through the eyes of the wounded , self-pitying child.

Release me from the strange mixture of the self-promoting hero and the imprisoned victim. Thank you that truth sets us free. Amen

FIG LEAF OF PREVIOUS ACHIEVEMENTS

In Joshua chapter 7, Joshua sends spies from Jericho to Ai, meaning 'The Ruin.' They return and report, 'Don't bother sending a lot of people - two or three thousand are enough to defeat Ai. Don't wear out the whole army, there aren't many people there.' Joshua had just experienced the spectacular Jericho victory so he listened to these reports without first consulting with God, all the more poignant when you consider that when he had been sent to spy out the Promised Land he and Caleb had not been listened to but the other spies were listened to in direct contrast to the word of God. Here Joshua relied on the strength of his army to defeat the small city but was defeated instead. Too often we rely on or hide behind our own skills, strength and expertise. Joshua hid behind his previous achievements and the report of the spies.

One man, Anthony, who came to me for prayer concerning his failing marriage and business, was not able to turn to God and honestly express his needs. Instead, in an attempt to bolster himself and avoid his feelings of inadequacy he would be self-promoting often reminding God of previous achievements. He would say, 'I've done it once (built a successful business) so I can do it again'!

Contrast this with Joshua who in essence pours out his true feelings to God. Afraid and confused he both complains and worries about God's reputation.

> '*Joshua and the elders of Israel tore their clothing in dismay, threw dust on their heads, and bowed face down to the ground before the Ark of the LORD until evening. Then Joshua cried out, "Oh, Sovereign LORD, why did you bring us across the Jordan River if you are going to let the Amorites kill us? If only we had been content to stay on the other side! Lord, what can I say now that Israel has fled from its enemies? For when the Canaanites and all the other people living in the land hear about it, they will surround us and wipe our name off the face of the earth. And then what will happen to the honour of your great name?"*' (Joshua 7:6-9)

God then answers by telling him to stop groveling and to stand up. He explains that Israel has sinned and that Joshua must deal with it. What follows is success.

When we avoid coming to God in honest confession we either, like Anthony, continue in self-promoting self-effort or we continually re-visit the situation internally or with friends. Why did God let it happen?- blaming God. Why did I do it?-blaming self. Why didn't I leave the situation as it was?- regret without repentance. Now everyone will know - catasrophizing. Going round in circles of despair and regret. What we need to do is be like Joshua – be honest with our feelings and failings – and talk to God.

I have left the aspect of the sin of deception until last in this chapter because I feel this is usually the only aspect of hiding and sin we think about.

PRAYER FOR REMOVING THE FIG LEAF OF PREVIOUS

ACHIEVEMENTS/FAILURES

Father, I pray you will release me from being locked in the past. Help me to stop hiding behind previous achievements, the 'self-made man', the 'I did it my way' person. Give me the courage to come before you naked and acknowledging my dependence on you.

Also Father, help me lay down the self-torturing thoughts concerning past failures and decisions. Release me from being stuck in that 'if only' place that stops me from taking responsibility in the present.

Help me to be truthful about where I am now and come to you for help. Amen

THE FIG LEAF OF DECEPTION

Whilst all hiding is sinful, the consequences do not always bring about death, but two prominent Bible stories illustrate how dangerous not only to ourselves, but to our whole Christian community, lying can be.

As we have been reading, Joshua 7 is about defeat. It is in fact the first defeat of the Children of Israel in the Promised Land, a defeat of the small city of Ai which leads to an army paralysed with fear, confused leaders and the destruction of a family. Following Joshua's prayer, God speaks to Joshua saying: -

> '*Israel has sinned and broken my covenant! They have stolen some of the things that I commanded must be set apart for me. And they have not only stolen them but have lied about it and hidden the things among their own belongings.*' (Joshua 7 v 11)

Joshua, by process of elimination confronts Achan, who is guilty. Achan's hiding of the stolen, forbidden possessions has devastating results. Achan follows the disastrous route that so many of us are tempted by. He saw beautiful treasures; he coveted them, stole them, hid them and lied. In so doing he separated himself from the community and allowed the love of the world's goods to squeeze out receiving the love of the Father. How often do we buy things we can't afford and then hide them from ourselves or our partners? Or lie about how much they cost? Are we totally honest with our tax returns or our benefit claims? How good are we at sorting out supermarket bills when we have been undercharged?

How often do we hide behind our new outfit, car or some household acquisition to make ourselves feel better or eligible? The desire to own the right thing in order to hide our fear of not being okay or acceptable is one of the enemy's seductions causing us to believe God is not enough.

It is worth noting that Achan came from a prominent family in Judah (1 Chronicles 2:47), so it was not poverty that drove him to take the forbidden things. His sin was not the mere act of keeping some of the booty (which was allowed in some cases) but his disobedience to God's command connected with this city.

118

Achan and his family were stoned in the Valley of Achor, named 'the Valley of Trouble.' This would become, in the grace of God, the Door of Hope (Hosea 2:15), the promise that God will bring restoration, healing and deliverance.

'I'll give her bouquets of roses. I'll turn Heartbreak Valley into Acres of Hope. She'll respond like she did as a young girl, those days when she was fresh out of Egypt.' (The Message).

The first recorded sin in the life of the New Testament Church involved two people hiding money, lying and pretending to be something they were not (Acts 5:1-11 NIV).

'Now a man named Ananias, together with his wife Sapphira, also sold a piece of property. With his wife's full knowledge he kept back part of the money for himself, but brought the rest and put it at the apostles' feet.

Then Peter said, "Ananias, how is it that Satan has so filled your heart that you have lied to the Holy Spirit and have kept for yourself some of the money you received for the land? Didn't it belong to you before it was sold? And after it was sold, wasn't the money at your disposal? What made you think of doing such a thing? You have not lied just to human beings but to God." When Ananias heard this, he fell down and died. And great fear seized all who heard what had happened. Then some young men came forward, wrapped up his body, and carried him out and buried him.

About three hours later his wife came in, not knowing what had happened. Peter asked her, "Tell me, is this the price you and Ananias got for the land?"

"Yes," she said, "that is the price."

Peter said to her, "How could you conspire to test the Spirit of the Lord? Listen! The feet of the men who buried your husband are at the door, and they will carry you out also."

At that moment she fell down at his feet and died. Then the young men came in and, finding her dead, carried her out and buried her beside her husband. Great fear seized

the whole church and all who heard about these events.'

It seems that Ananias and Sapphira were bound by their desire for approval or acclaim. They couldn't give in freedom and honesty as led by the Holy Spirit but rather needed to use the giving to increase their reputation. They wanted to appear more generous than they were in reality, prepared to be and they wanted to be admired. (They could have kept the field, given half, whatever). So often we are like Ananias and Sapphira - afraid of being rejected or shamed by others if we admit to weakness or failure, but the resulting cover-up can isolate people from each other and the healing power of the Christian community. Selling fields isn't really an issue today, but how many of us would be prepared to tell our small group how much or little we earn, for instance, or talk about our teenagers' problems or marriage difficulties? We need to choose to be known so we have nothing to hide. We need to know God and be known by God, then in the security of His knowing us we need to be known by each other.

Not only do we deceive others, we deceive ourselves. We need to be able to tell/write out our life story as truthfully as possible. It takes more than one attempt! Sometimes we want to enhance our achievements, other times we tell our story from the wounded self-pitying child.

1 John 1:8 says, '*If we say that we have no sin we deceive ourselves and the truth is not in us.*' Isaiah 1:18 says, '*"Come now, let us reason together"*, says the Lord, "*though your sins are as scarlet they shall be white as snow.*"' This needs always to be part of our everyday living.

One pastor came to see me whose ability to deceive himself and not connect to his sinful actions was extreme. Maurice had been brought up in South America by a very harsh, successful missionary father. Whenever, as a child, he 'sinned', often for childish misdemeanours that he was unaware of, his father made him kneel before a cross on a cold stone floor in a darkened room. There he was told to confess his sins to the Lord Jesus and not leave the room until he knew God had forgiven him. At first Maurice said that, as a four or five-year-old, he would spend hours in there, fearful that God had not forgiven him. However, after a few years he began to just pay lip service to this punishment and in a detached way 'confess', stay a while and leave.

I had been asked to see Maurice by his bishop. Maurice had been on a healing weekend and one of the sessions had involved confessing your sins to a prayer minister. Maurice confessed to two adulterous affairs and an ongoing sexual relationship with his curate. The prayer minister suggested he needed to tell his wife. He went home, wrote a confessional note to his wife and left to preach at the evening service. (The wife then rang the Bishop). He was so cut off from his emotions and his actions that he was not able to make any connection. Our levels of deception are not normally this extreme. However, quoting Andy Comiskey:

'In fact the fig leaf which covers the sin endangers souls more than sin itself. At Desert Stream the most powerful temptation faced by staff and participants alike is not sexual immorality itself but the love of hiding the sin or struggle. False piety, not overt sin, is our greatest enemy.'[36]

Dallas Willard says in his book The Spirit of the Disciplines: 'There is a deep longing among Christians and non-Christians alike for the personal purity and power to live as our hearts tell us we should.'[37] Living the authentic Christian life is about learning how to do that, making our insides match our outsides. The Bible says we can only do that in the context of a Biblical, loving community. We need the Church, as Christian brothers and sisters, to help us to become truly authentic people.

Wherever we are in our spiritual journey we need to see authenticity, which is defined as 'That which is trustworthy, reliable and genuine' - as a life-changing, life-guiding principle. How do we do this? There are two principles, as well as private confession and confession to one another, we need to belong to a group of people who accept us where we are but who love us enough to encourage support and believe for change (See Chapter 7). The acceptance that we are growing, changing, 'becoming' people, that we are not the person we were last year but neither the person we are going to be next year. Indeed, we all need to be able to accept that we are changing people and give ourselves and others the space to change and to become.

Part of my healing was hearing John Wimber say before 4,000 people (he was talking about some theological view) 'Well, that is what I am thinking this year. I may have changed my mind by next year.' How amazing! You can actually speak on the subject without having it written in tablets of stone, whereas in my family whatever decision you made was forever, it was seen as an act of extreme betrayal and disloyalty if you changed your mind.

This is why I think people find Christmas so difficult in unhealthy families, because on returning home we may hear statements like, 'Well, you never used to think that, dear' or 'You've changed, you're not the person I know.' 'You've always arrived on Christmas Eve before, so that's when we were expecting to see you.......' Change is never viewed as positive. So part of our difficulty is learning that we are 'becoming people',

'works in progress' that as Christians we are meant to be
continually changing to be more like Jesus, or in John
Townsend's language 'We are unfinished people'. [38]

As I keep emphasizing in this Chapter, we need to choose to
be known. We need to know God and to be known by God. Then
in the security of His knowing us we can find the courage to be
known by each other. Holiness is not just how we are with God
but how we live this out with each other. In order to risk this we
need to be able to trust God's *character,* that He is good and
that what He says is true. Adam and Eve's inability to do this
led, of course, to them eating the apple and covering themselves
with fig leaves.

'*The next day as they were leaving Bethany, Jesus was
hungry. Seeing in the distance a fig tree in leaf, he went to
find out if it had any fruit. When he reached it, he found
nothing but leaves, because it was not the season for figs.
Then he said to the tree, "May no one ever eat fruit from
you again." And his disciples heard him say it.*' (Mark
11:12-14 NIV)

'In the morning, as they went along, they saw the fig tree withered from the roots. Peter remembered and said to Jesus, "Rabbi, look! The fig tree you cursed has withered!"' (Mark 11:20-21 NIV)

This incident is understood to be an 'acted-out' parable. Jesus has already visited the temple (Mark 11:11) on his arrival in Jerusalem. Then he had spent the night with his disciples in Bethany a couple of miles outside the city. The next day on their return to the temple (this is when Jesus overturned the tables) the story of the cursing of the fig tree takes place. Most Bible footnotes and commentaries see this as a metaphor for Israel and those people claiming to be God's people but who do not bear fruit for him.

However, I have often wondered if it is symbolic, like the tearing of the temple veil. The temple curtain separating the Holy Place from the Holy of Holies was split in two at Christ's death, symbolising that the barrier between God and His people was removed. Maybe the cursing of the fig tree symbolized the

ending of our separation and hiding from God, from ourselves
and from each other.

For some of us, however, our fig leaves have become part
of us and so in order to come out of hiding we must be like
Eustace in the *Voyage of the Dawn Treader and* be
'undragoned.' Eustace hated everybody and everybody hated
him. He did not believe his cousins' accounts of Narnia so he
teased and bullied them but he finds himself magically on a
boat, the *Dawn Treader,* taking a great voyage. At one point
this boat pulls in to an island and Eustace wanders off and
finds a cave. The cave proves to be filled with diamonds and
rubies and gold. He thinks 'I'm rich!' and immediately, because
he is who he is, he thinks that now he'll be able to pay
everybody back: anyone who has laughed at him, stepped on
him, slighted him, will now get their comeuppance. Eustace
then falls asleep on the pile of treasure - which he doesn't yet
know is the hoard of a dragon - and because he falls asleep with
greedy, dragonish thoughts in his heart, when he wakes up
he's become a dragon -big, terrible and ugly. Soon he realizes

there's no way out. He can't go on the boat, he's going to be left on the island alone, he's going to be horrible all of his life.

He realizes how lonely it is to be a monster, he starts to understand what sort of person he is and begins to weep. Aslan comes; Eustace follows him to a well where Aslan directs him to take off his dragon suit. He manages to do this and then steps into the water only to see a smaller dragon suit, and then another. He is desperate after the third attempt, so the Lion says, 'You will have to let me undress you.' Eustace is frightened of the Lion's claws, which go very deep, right through Eustace's heart but he agrees. Then the Lion throws him into the crystal water, which smarts at first, but then Eustace surfaces from the delicious water, finding himself to be a boy again.

Like Eustace, we cannot change ourselves. We have to allow God to come and undragon us. Of course we always want to run, hide and to avoid any pain.

PRAYER FOR REMOVING THE FIG LEAF OF DECEPTION

If we confess our sins, God is faithful to forgive us our sins and cleanse us from all unrighteousness. (1 John 1:9)

Father, forgive me where I lie, pretend, cover up and where I am not truthful. Help me to risk honesty. Give me the courage to be vulnerable, transparent and authentic. Help me to stop struggling to hold onto things, to hide.

Give me a glimpse of loving community I pray, so that I will realize the isolation of deception really isn't worth the cost. Bring me out into your glorious healing Presence where I can begin to live with my sisters and brothers. Amen

PRAYER TO BE 'UNDRAGONED'

Father God, I come to You as someone who is tired of my own self-effort. I confess that I have become that which You did not intend me to be. I have allowed my sinful thoughts to poison me, causing me to shrivel on the inside. I have believed my own self-promotion and became image without substance. I am fearful of the pain of being set free. I am fearful that I will barely exist. Yet I cry out to You.

Please come and remove these false personality images and pretending I have laboured under. Wash me clean, heal me and breathe resurrected life into my true personhood, the 'all that you have called me to be' person. Amen.

Take off our rags for the garments of splendor. Isaiah 52:1-2

THE RAGMAN adapted from "Ragman and Other Cries of Faith"
by Walter Wangerin Jr.,

'Before dawn one Friday morning I noticed a man, handsome and strong. He was pulling an old cart filled with clothes both bright and new, and he was calling in a clear voice: "Rags! New rags for old! I take your tired rags! Rags!

"Now, this is a wonder," I thought to myself, for the man stood six-feet-four, his arms were like tree limbs, hard and muscular, and his eyes flashed intelligence. Could he find no better job than to be a ragman in the inner city? I followed him. My curiosity drove me, and I wasn't disappointed.

Soon the Ragman saw a woman sitting on her back porch. She was sobbing into a handkerchief, sighing, and shedding a thousand tears. Her shoulders shook. Her heart was breaking. The Ragman stopped his cart. Quietly, he walked to the woman. "Give me your rag," he said gently, "and I'll give you another." He slipped the handkerchief from her eyes. She looked up, and he laid across her palm a linen cloth so clean and new that it shined. She blinked from the gift to the giver. Then, as he began to pull his cart again, the Ragman did a strange thing; He put her stained handkerchief to his own face; and then HE began to weep, to sob as grievously as she had done, his shoulders shaking. Yet she was left without a tear.

"What a wonder," I sighed as I followed the sobbing Ragman. "Rags! Rags! New rags for old!"

In a little while, the Ragman came upon a girl whose head was wrapped in a bandage, whose eyes were empty. Blood soaked her bandage. A line of blood ran down her cheek. The Ragman looked upon this child with pity, and he drew a lovely yellow bonnet from his cart. "Give me your rag," he said, and I'll give you mine."

The child could only gaze at him while he loosened the bandage, removed it, and tied it to his own head. The bonnet he set on hers. With the bandage went the wound! Across his brow ran darker, more substantial blood - his own!

"Rags! Rags! I take old rags!" cried the sobbing, bleeding, strong, intelligent Ragman.

"Are you going to work?" he asked a man who leaned against a telephone pole. The man shook his head. The Ragman pressed him: "Do you have a job?" "Are you crazy?" sneered the other. He pulled away from the pole, revealing the right sleeve of his jacket - flat, the cuff stuffed into the pocket. He had no arm.

"So," said the Ragman. "Give me your jacket, and I'll give you mine." Such quiet authority in his voice!

The one-armed man took off his jacket. So did the Ragman - and the Ragman's arm stayed in its sleeve. When the other put it on he had two good arms, thick as tree limbs; but the Ragman had only one. "Go to work," he said.

After that he found a drunk, lying unconscious beneath an army blanket, an old man, hunched, wizened, and sick. He took the army blanket and wrapped it round himself, but for the drunk he left new clothes and a new blanket.

And now I had to run to keep up with the Ragman. Though he was weeping uncontrollably, and bleeding freely at the forehead, pulling his cart with one arm, falling again and again, exhausted, old, old, and sick, yet he went with haste.

I wept to see the change in the Ragman. I hurt to see his sorrow. And yet I needed to see where he was going in such haste, perhaps to know what drove him so.

The little old Ragman came to a landfill, to the garbage pits. I wanted to help him in what he did, but I hung back, hiding. He climbed a hill. With tormented labour he cleared a little space, sighed, lay down, and pillowed his head on a

handkerchief and a jacket. He covered his bones with an
army blanket.

And he died. Oh, how I cried to witness that death!

I slumped into a junked car and wailed and mourned
as one who has no hope - because I had come to love the
Ragman. Every other face had faded in the wonder of this
wonderful man, and I cherished him; but he died.

I sobbed myself to sleep. I did not know - how could I
know? - that I slept through Friday night and Saturday
and its night, too.

But then, on Sunday morning, I was wakened by a pure,
hard, demanding light. It slammed against my sour face. I
blinked, I looked, and I saw the last and the first wonder
of all.

There was the Ragman, carefully folding the blanket, a
scar on his forehead, but alive and healthy! There was no
sign of sorrow or of age. The rags that he had gathered
shined for cleanliness.

I lowered my head and trembling for all that I had seen, I myself walked up to the Ragman. I told him my name with shame, for I was a sorry figure next to him. Then I took off all my clothes in that place, and I said to him with yearning in my voice: "Dress me." He dressed me.

My Lord, he put new rags on me, and I am a wonder beside him. I am His Bride! '

4

It is not unusual to become stuck in painful circumstances without the understanding of how to move forward. So I have decided to write about disappointment and suffering as another layer to be unwrapped before we can receive the gift of confession.

Psalm 102:1-11, 23-28 are passages that form a prayer for help. It is a prayer to an eternal King.

> 'LORD, hear my prayer! Listen to my plea! Don't turn away from me in my time of distress. Bend down to listen, and answer me quickly when I call to you.
> For my days disappear like smoke, and my bones burn like red-hot coals. My heart is sick, withered like grass, and I have lost my appetite.
> Because of my groaning, I am reduced to skin and bones. I am like an owl in the desert, like a little owl in a far-off wilderness. I lie awake, lonely as a solitary bird on the

roof.

My enemies taunt me day after day. They mock and curse me. I eat ashes for food. My tears run down into my drink because of your anger and wrath. For you have picked me up and thrown me out. My life passes as swiftly as the evening shadows. I am withering away like grass.

He broke my strength in midlife, cutting short my days. But I cried to him, "O my God, who lives forever, don't take my life while I am so young"!
Long ago you laid the foundation of the earth and made the heavens with your hands. They will perish, but you remain forever; they will wear out like old clothing. You will change them like a garment and discard them.
But you are always the same; you will live forever. The children of your people
will live in security. Their children's children will thrive in your presence.'

We can feel disillusioned, troubled, overwhelmed or exhausted. We can be heavyhearted, sick with the events of life - beaten down or just disappointed.

DISAPPOINTMENT

One of my favourite movies is `It's a Wonderful Life`. This film classic tells the story of George Bailey, a promising young man with a good heart who wants desperately to leave his home town to find success in the world. He has dreams that are too big for little Bedford Falls. But circumstances keep getting in the way. The Army rejects him because he has a hearing problem. His father's death forces him to take over management of the family's Building and Loan Association. A run on the bank soaks up his savings, preventing him from leaving Bedford Falls even for his honeymoon. Try as he might, he cannot escape. But he makes the best of it because he is a good man. He settles down, marries his high school sweetheart, and raises a family. But more, he serves the community by loaning money to poor people so they can buy homes and he shows generosity to everyone. He gives up his big dreams to live a little life well, though he never gets over feeling just a tinge of disappointment.

A crisis in the family business, however, caused by an inadvertently misplaced envelope, pushes him over the edge. He feels crushed by how his life has turned out, and he momentarily forgets what has made his life meaningful. He is about to end his life when an angel, Clarence, intervenes. Clarence gives George a precious gift. He lets George see what would have happened if he had never lived at all and what would have become of Bedford Falls without him. Clarence finally says to him, "You've been given a great gift, George, a chance to see what the world would be like without you..... Strange, isn't it? Each man's life touches so many other lives. When he isn't around he leaves an awful hole, doesn't he?...... You see, George, you really had a wonderful life. Don't you see what a mistake it would be to throw it away?" George's life was good because he chose to make it good, in spite of and perhaps because of the disappointments he faced along the way. He made the best of bad situations and was faithful to what he knew was right.

Disappointments are something we all live with, but how we see them is important. God spoke to me saying that our disappointments are our battle wounds, our battle scars. When God spoke to me concerning this I remembered a church I had been speaking at the previous month. Often when I am teaching on prayer ministry I will speak about unanswered prayers and ask people to stand who need the Holy Spirit's touch where through unanswered prayers or broken dreams there is an ongoing disappointment. Normally about sixty percent of the group will stand. In this particular church however, the response was only about ten percent. So when God spoke about disappointments being our battle scars, I asked about this church and God replied, "The church had desired little and prayed less."

Disappointment is often a consequence of embracing life and risking, rather than protecting ourselves and staying safe. So when disappointments come either with God, life or ourselves we can grow tired of waiting for the better times: - we can lose hope and live in grey bitter resignation or we can acknowledge the truth that life is difficult. This is difficult.

Morgan Scott Peck, an American Christian psychiatrist states in his book '*Life is DIFFICULT.*'[39]

This is a great truth because until we understand this we moan about our problems and our burdens as though life should be easy.

We can also believe, somewhat narcissistically, that these problems have been personally sent upon us, that they are unique to either us or our family, class or race and others don't experience these or any other difficulties.

Happiness is not an avoidance of sin and suffering or disappointment! It is discovering God's way to live when there is pain and suffering. It's practising life skills that keep us connected to God, ourselves and others in healthy ways instead of defaulting to our survival techniques or 'fig leaves', which cause us to hide from Him.

So much of our disappointment is linked to our own wounded misinterpretation or our assumptions concerning what people are promising or what the Gospel says.

I was always disappointed with my own life because I was always waiting to get there - wherever there was. I practised the magical thinking of 'somewhere over the rainbow,' so when I became a Christian I had unrealistic expectations of heaven here on earth, and without the healing to transform this into godly hope, I became disappointed.

We can misunderstand what words mean and think peace equals 'nothing troublesome will ever happen to me again.' 'Joy' can be misinterpreted as 'I will only experience things that make me happy,' or 'Jesus will never leave you' means 'I will never feel lonely again,' and when life doesn't work out as we expect, we feel disappointed.

We often expect Jesus to behave in a certain way or answer our prayers according to our plan. We experience confusion and disappointment when things do not work out how we thought they would.

I imagine John the Baptist may have felt this, he had recognised Jesus as the 'Lamb of God' and probably in that revelation understood a great deal about Jesus' mission. Yet

Jesus, the one who had come to set the prisoners free (Luke 4:18) did not release him from prison.

> 'The next day John saw Jesus coming toward him and said, "Look! The Lamb of God who takes away the sin of the world! He is the one I was talking about when I said, 'A man is coming after me who is far greater than I am, for he existed long before me.'(John 1:29-30)

We can have unrealistic expectations of the church, church leaders and ourselves which cause us to blame God, others or ourselves. Blame is often a legitimate desire for truth, justice and something better whilst protecting ourselves from any shame, responsibility and sin.

Yes, church is very often disappointing. There can be a credibility gap between what is said and what happens. Church can often talk about love and family but behave more like an organisation. Church can talk about loving one another whilst being too busy to make friends. As a result of this we can remain stuck with a miserable existence of self-pity and blaming, or in my case wrongly taking responsibility for everything.

Alternatively, we can turn to God and ask Him to give us creative ideas.

One recently widowed lady spoke to me about how she missed cooking and eating a Sunday roast. Cooking and eating a roast dinner for one isn't very practical. A few months later when I met her she told me how once a month she invites some of the singles and widows from her church to Sunday lunch. They start with sherry then a glass of wine with their meal, pudding and coffee, quite a feast! At Christmas, having just lost her husband she went and helped out in the Salvation Army. Next Christmas she may be providing a Christmas lunch at her own church. Of course she still misses her husband and experiences sorrow, loneliness and tears, but in one area where she can bring about change she co-operated with God's creative life-giving idea.

We can also have misunderstanding about prayer and deep disappointment concerning unanswered prayer. So often we treat God like a computer where if only we could find the right keys, type in the correct request, we would get all the answers and information on the screen. We think that if we spent

enough time and energy looking we would have the formula for

successful living. This all leads to frustration and

disappointment. We end up disappointed with God or with

ourselves because we wrongly believe we have failed or been

unable to pray correctly. God is interested in us and in having a

relationship with us. The all-powerful Creator of the Universe

wants to be a Father to us. Likewise, we can have problems with

our concept of faith, falsely believing our faith has to be as big

as our problems. It's where we put our faith that counts - or to

be more precise in *whom* we put our faith. When we put our

faith in God rather than in how much faith we do or don't have

we are looking to a mighty warrior, the King of Kings who is also

our Father. According to the book of Hebrews, faith is the

assurance of things hoped for, the conviction of things not seen.

Our immediate circumstances may not provide evidence of God's

existence, so our provision of faith helps us to see spiritual

reality beyond our physical sight. We can be imprisoned by

many different circumstances but Jesus comes to set the

prisoners free. What does this freedom look like whereby we can say despite the circumstances, 'My chains fell off; my heart is set free.' The paradox is we somehow live both sides of the cross. The following poem expresses this well.

No Scar

Has thou no scar?

No hidden scar on foot, or side or hand? I hear thee
sung as mighty in the land; I hear them hail thy bright
ascendant star. Hast thou no scar?

Has thou no wound?

Yet I was wounded by the archers, spent,

Leaned me against a tree to die;

And rent by ravening beasts that encompassed me,

I swooned:

Hast thou no wound?

No wound? No scar?

Yet, as Master shall the servant be,

And pierced are the feet that follow me;

But thine are whole;

Can he have followed far

Who has no wound or scar?

Amy Wilson Carmichael

Prayer for the Healing of Disappointment

Father God, I release to you my disappointment. I understand I have spiritualised my rose coloured spectacles and much of my view of life has been magical thinking rather than faith. I am sorry for all the times I have compared my life as it is with the life I fantasised, or hoped for in the future, and have felt disappointed. Please forgive and heal me.

Father, I ask for healing where I have subtly put my faith in *faith* rather than in *You*. I have looked for a formula to get my answers rather than sought your presence and I am sorry.

I lift to you all my unanswered prayers and broken dreams and ask for a gift of trust and hope. Help me to see beyond this painful place and to believe for the "what is yet to be." Amen

MAKING SENSE OF SUFFERING

Rick Richardson writes, 'In some ways Jesus lessens the man's pain and suffering, but in other ways Jesus puts him in a position to suffer and feel pain even more. Healing is not primarily about escape or relief from pain, at least as Jesus practiced it. This is a great challenge to us: I think most people pursue their own healing and minister healing to others with the primary goal of finding relief and release from pain. That's the wrong goal, at least from a Biblical perspective. Healing is primarily about the transformation of the person into a truer and more whole follower, worshipper and lover of God.

Sometimes the healing journey raises us up on to mountain tops, where we feel the sun and the wind, the exuberant joy of wider horizons and clearer perspective. And sometimes the healing journey leads us through the shadow of death, the valley of loneliness and darkness. In the end we are transformed to be like the One who healed us. But at points along the way our pain and darkness may increase as we take a turn towards wholeness.' [40]

At this point do we turn outward or hide? Do we blame ourselves or someone else? Do we become stuck in complaining, anger, resentment or bitterness? Or do we trust?

Loneliness, darkness, pain and suffering are part of our life's journey, but we have a choice as to how we respond to these difficulties.

1 Peter 5:10

`And the God of all grace, who called you to his eternal glory in Christ, after you have suffered a little while, will himself restore you and make you strong, firm and steadfast.'

When Bad Things Happen to Good People

After relocating his family to Boston, Massachusetts, Rabbi Harold Kushner was informed by a local paediatrician that his three-year-old son, Aaron, would never grow taller than 3 feet and would suffer the symptoms of Progeria ('rapid ageing'). This news threw his entire belief about God out of the window. He would go on to wonder how a God that he had been so loyal to could do such a terrible thing to him. Rabbi Kushner went on to make it his life's work to explore 'When bad things happen to good people'. This is an extreme example, but we all suffer blows in life that seem unfair. It seems to be the case that nature doesn't discriminate between good and bad, the faithful and the faithless, the criminals and the saints. Otherwise, why do bad things happen to good people? Why does an entire village get wiped out in a hurricane? Were all those people bad? Why does a mother lose her son to an untimely death? Why do innocent people die or get injured as they collide with a drunk driver?

When bad things happen to good people, sometimes people find solace in turning to God. Others turn away. We may bargain with God, if I pray and go to church will you protect me from anymore suffering? We may just fall into deep depression with a fatalist view saying, 'Life isn't fair, it's never been fair to me and it never will be.' Having something bad happen doesn't mean

God doesn't exist. It just means that we don't know why bad things happen to good people. The temptation is too respond with Christian platitudes or guesswork, so I think the question isn't 'Why do bad things happen to good people', the question is more aptly, 'What do we do when bad things happen to good people?' [41]

When bad things happen, sometimes we think we are being punished in some way. One lady before she was married had an abortion. Once she was married she had two healthy babies and then a miscarriage. Despite all the good things that had happened she believed her miscarriage was a punishment from God for the abortion. This erroneous belief is not uncommon and is well illustrated in the bible.

When Joseph's brothers travelled to Egypt for food, Joseph accused them of being spies and put them in prison for three days. Then he released all of them except Simeon, telling them to return for their younger brother. Their response was:

> 'They said to one another, "Surely we are being punished because of our brother. We saw how distressed

he was when he pleaded with us for his life, but we would

not listen; that's why this distress has come on us."

Reuben replied, "Didn't I tell you not to sin against the

boy? But you wouldn't listen! Now we must give an

accounting for his blood."' (Genesis 42:21-22 NIV).

Later in the story, when Joseph accuses Benjamin of stealing the cup, Judah replies:

'"*What can we say to my lord?" "What can we say?*

How can we prove our innocence? God has uncovered

your servants' guilt. We are now my lord's slaves - we

ourselves and the one who was found to have the cup."'

(Genesis 44:16)

When trying to make sense of bad things we often blame ourselves. Also, when the effects of trauma linger longer than we feel they should we think there is something wrong with us, leading to greater shame and disappointment. For example, we may wonder why we still cry many years after the traumatic event. We don't understand we are stuck in the pain of the past, so we judge ourselves. The neural circuitry that got fused

155

together during that trauma is still fused together, so there's nothing wrong with the tears, it's just automatic. We need God's healing, but the judgements we make get in the way of receiving it. It's natural to cry when we are in pain. Allowing ourselves to feel the emotion can actually nurture self-compassion and self- acceptance. Tears are a God-given gift.

Disappointment leads people to accommodate the status quo. But we have a choice, we can adjust our theology to make room for prayers not being answered and allow our experience to define our view of God and of scripture, or we can take our pain, suffering and lamentations to God. We can see the latter approach in the story of Stephen.

Acts 6 begins with the apostles' selection of seven people 'of good reputation, full of the Spirit and of wisdom' to serve widows at the early church version of a soup kitchen. This leaves the apostles free for prayer and ministry of the Word, so they lay hands on these seven to serve. Stephen is described as 'full of grace and power, performing great wonders and signs among the people' (verse 8). Then immediately in Acts 7 he preaches a mega-sermon that enrages his audience to such an extent that they stone him to death, and widespread persecution of Jesus' follower's results. It was such a big blow to these first Christians who had already been through so many devastating disappointments. Jesus' betrayal by one of their own and his arrest and execution were fresh in their memories. His resurrection certainly brought radical hope, but Jesus then left them in his ascension.

Acts 5 had ended with the apostles going away from a flogging rejoicing that they had been considered worthy to suffer shame for his name. But now, following Stephen's story there is martyrdom, unprecedented persecution that scatters the remaining six table servers throughout Judea and Samaria, leading to house-to-house searches, arrests and imprisonment.

Then in the middle of this we read Acts 8:2, '*some devout people buried Stephen, and made loud lamentations over him.*'

Lamentation, the public and private expressions of pain and suffering, is essential. It's important to note that lamentation is not a technique that guarantees immediate breakthrough. After loudly lamenting Stephen's death, things don't get immediately better; we see that Saul is part of the house-to-house searches dragging people off to prison (8:3). In the next story, however, Philip, the second person ordained to care for widows, flees to Samaria where crowds hear his preaching and see miraculous signs. [42]

Rabbi Kushner, of whom I wrote earlier, argues in his book 'When Bad Things Happen to Good People' that we should accept God's love but downgrade our expectations of His power. Carl Jung in his book, 'An Answer to Job', written seven years after the last world war, questions God's goodness. Hudson Taylor, a known missionary to China, moved to Switzerland on doctor's orders in a state of complete mental breakdown. There he heard the terrible news that 58 of his fellow missionaries and 21 children had been massacred in the Boxer Revolution. It was almost more than he could bear. He admitted to his wife, 'I cannot read, I cannot think, I cannot even pray - but I can trust.' His trust was well-founded. The blood of such martyrs was to become the seed of the Chinese church, one of the most vibrant and sacrificial in the modern world. You see, what

Kushner, (a Jew) and Jung, (an occultist), did not see, is that one ultimate miracle - the resurrection of the Son of God from the dead! This assures us that every buried dream and dashed hope will ultimately be absorbed and resurrected into a reality far greater than anything we can currently imagine. Unanswered prayer is only difficult for us who truly believe. For cynics it is simply a reassurance that they were right all along. To struggle is faith!

Blaise Pascal, in *Pensees*, concludes that believers are the truest sceptics because they have to align everything that happens to them to the concept of a good God.

So what should our attitude be when things do go wrong? Very often the thought is, 'It's not fair!' One of the first things we need to understand is that things DO go wrong. Life is unfair and unless we realise this we are stuck in a place of immaturity, separate from God and hidden in our own self-pity, pain and bitterness. The question, therefore, is not 'Will I suffer'? but rather, 'How will I suffer'? We need to decide what will be my attitude to life in general and God's will for my life?

Children believe that good things happen to good people and bad things happen to bad people. We can continue to believe this in subtle forms as an adult, so one of the questions we have to tackle is our own negative self-image. We can often be caught in the trap of believing the lie that if things have gone wrong it must be because we are bad. The other questions are concerning God. Why did He let it happen? Where was He? Does He care? Can't He help? Faced with the tension between God's love and God's omnipotence we may decide to accept God's love but then downgrade our expectations of His power. Alternatively, we insist that God, by definition, must be omnipotent, so then we doubt His goodness.

Thomas a Kempis dealt realistically with life's difficulties when he wrote:

'The days of this life are short and evil, full of sorrow and misery, where a person is stained with many sins, ensnared by many passions, bound by many fears, swollen by many cares, distracted by many curiosities, entangled by many vanities, surrounded by many

160

mistakes, weakened by many efforts, weighed down by temptations, stained by pleasures, tormented by wants. Oh, when will there be an end to all these things that have gone awry in God's plan? [43]

Where is God in all this suffering? Christians have pondered this question for centuries. It seems as if God has either power but no love, or love but no power. But if God has both power and love, muscle and heart [44], we could say 'Why do innocent people suffer? Where is God's muscle and heart when we need them'?

So much of our problem with suffering is because it raises these perplexing questions about God's character and plan.

Suffering appears to run contrary to the will of God. God created the world as a good place. Life as we live it now is not the way it's supposed to be, nor the way God designed it to be. Our abhorrence of suffering reflects a God-given impulse that runs deep within our nature. We recoil before suffering, not only because we dislike the pain, but also because we realise instinctively that we were not made for suffering. It is a violation of God's creational intent. Life should not be like this! I should not be struggling/suffering like this.

The disciples on the Emmaus Road had difficulty recognising Jesus. I believe they were looking for the wrong Messiah. We have the paradox of both the suffering servant - Jesus on the Cross - and the victorious, resurrected Lord! A crucified Messiah was an oxymoron, a contradictory theology.

In the film *Grand Canyon* an immigration attorney breaks out of a traffic jam and attempts to bypass it. His route takes him along streets that seem progressively darker and more deserted. Then the predictable happens - his expensive car stalls on one of those alarming streets whose teenage guardians favour expensive guns and knives. The attorney does manage to phone for a pickup truck, but before it arrives, five young gang members surround his disabled car and threaten him with considerable bodily harm. Then, just in time, the tow truck shows up and its driver - an earnest, genial man - begins to hook up to the disabled car. The gang members protest: the truck driver is interrupting their enjoyment. So the driver takes the leader of the group aside and says:

> 'Man, the world ain't supposed to work like this. Maybe you don't know that, but this ain't the way it's supposed to be. I'm supposed to be able to do my job without askin' you if I can. And that dude is supposed to be able to wait with his car without you rippin' him off. Everything's supposed to be different than what it is here.'[45]

Now central to all our classic Christian understanding is the way things are supposed to be: a world designed and intended by God to be a beautiful creation, where we lived with authentic relationships and deep peace. And it is supposed to be fair.

When my children regularly announced, 'It's not fair', I would reply, 'Life's not fair'!

You will struggle with trying to make life fair! If it was, there would not be famine in Africa, and honest shopkeepers would not be gobbled up by supermarkets. People in the Third World wouldn't be asked for grossly inflated interest on their loans that they are unable to pay. Life is not fair, good things don't just happen to good people and bad things to bad people - life is not fair - but GOD IS JUST. Our desire for justice is God-given, so we live with all of the paradox. We think life should be fair because God is.

Prayer for Perseverance

Father God, help me to accept that life is difficult and not always fair. I ask for the wisdom to know what battles to fight. In those battles give me courage to stand against evil and injustice I pray. I ask for strength to fight the good fight.

But also Father, for wisdom to know those things I cannot change and to live with those things with love and compassion. May I, as Victor Hugo wrote, 'Have courage for the great sorrows of life and patience for the small ones and when you have the laboriously accomplished your daily tasks, go to sleep in peace, God is awake.'[46] Amen

However, whilst holding this hope in our hearts we need to release our resentment as to how things are. If we cling to 'This is how it should be' we'll struggle to feel content or satisfied unless it is exactly as we would like or want. How it is will never feel quite good enough and there will be no way of moving forward. When we are stuck like this we are unable to forgive or to take responsibility for our reactions of anger, bitterness and resentment and open the gift of confession.

When we hold strong views on how things should be, resent how they are or expect God to be who we think He should be, or to answer in a certain way, we block our hope. And 'hope deferred makes the heart sick'. Unrelenting disappointment leaves us heart-sick and bitter. '*Hope deferred makes the heart sick, but a longing fulfilled is a tree of life.*' (Proverbs 13:12 NIV)

When we are in this place of 'stuckness' we hold on to our resentment, disappointment and unanswered prayers. We blame, complain and often keep God at arms' length.

If we just hold strong views on how things should be or about what we expect we may be unwilling to accept another

166

outcome, however good. C. S. Lewis illustrates this in his novel Perelandra:

'What you have made me see', answered the Lady 'is as plain as the sky, but I never saw it before. Yet it has happened every day. One goes into the forest to pick food and already the thought of one fruit rather than another has grown up in one's mind. Then, maybe one finds a different fruit and not the fruit one thought of. One joy was expected and another is given. But this I had never noticed before that at the very moment of the finding there is in the mind a kind of thrusting back, or a setting aside. The picture of the fruit you have not found is still, for a moment, before you. And if you wished - if it were possible to wish - you could keep it there. You could send your soul after the good you had expected, instead of turning it to the good you had got. You could refuse the real good; you could make the real fruit taste insipid by thinking of the other.'

One can conceive a heart which did this, which clung to the good it had first thought of and turn the good which was given into no good.

It 'turned the good it had been given into no good' by comparing, and that is how we use our heart - a bitter complaint 'This is not what I expected, this is not how it should be' every time we turn to the 'if only'.

Mary, mother of Jesus, is a wonderful example of someone who did not cling to how it should be. First, in accepting her pregnancy......and years later she did not hang onto Jesus, but released Him and accepted John. [47]

'Standing near the cross were Jesus' mother, and his mother's sister, Mary (the wife of Clopas), and Mary Magdalene. When Jesus saw his mother standing there beside the disciple he loved, he said to her, "Dear woman, here is your son." And he said to this disciple, "Here is your mother." And from then on this disciple took her into his home.' (John 19:25-27)

As I have written, it is not 'will I suffer'? but 'how will I suffer'? Along with our stuckness with how things should be, we can be frozen in some moment in time because of loss or trauma. We may have feelings of having had our childhood stolen, abducted, kidnapped by neglect, abuse or deprivation. We think things like 'I have been short-changed', 'I was dealt a bad hand', 'This is my lot in life' or 'I am entitled to more than this.'

Benjamin Franklin is quoted as saying, 'Poverty often deprives a man of all spirit and virtue. It is hard for an empty bag to stand upright.'[48]

With God however, we can become upright again. Some part of us may be in darkness, stuck in a prison of our own making because we don't know how to stop punishing ourselves for something we have done. But we can come to God and confess, allowing Jesus to take the punishment.

Or maybe it is part of our adult life that has been stolen, and we are suffering because our hearts and souls have become corrupted by the seduction of the world, or our involvement in the occult. Also we can lose large parts of ourselves through the control of others or through their continuing criticism. Or we have imprisoned ourselves by our own lack of self-acceptance, believing the lie we are still an ugly duckling when we have grown into a swan. We can find ourselves living in a grey place where it is 'forever winter and never Christmas' [49]. The response to this is not to give up and subtly wear the armour of resistance keeping God, our church and Christian friends at arm's length. When we do this we find we get annoyed with others, not believing their experiences and God encounters. We decide more successful Christians at church are always exaggerating or have it easy. We become bad tempered, wrapping ourselves in bitter disappointment, hibernating and hiding in the darkness; but Jesus is saying, '*Come to the light.*' (Ephesians 5:14). '*Awake, sleeper, rise from the dead. Christ will give you light.*'

Unless we respond to Jesus, take responsibility for our sinful reactions and confess, we remain stuck in the darkness/greyness because we do not know how to stop punishing ourselves, or to stop nursing our bitter memories.

The bible has many stories of people like us responding sinfully to suffering. In Exodus we see the children of Israel blaming Moses – 'What are we going to drink. Have you brought us this far that we should die of thirst.'?

> `Then Moses led the people of Israel away from the Red Sea, and they moved out into the Shur Desert. They travelled in this desert for three days without water. When they came to Marah, they finally found water. But the people couldn't drink it because it was bitter. (That is why the place was called Marah, which means "bitter.") Then the people turned against Moses. "What are we going to drink?" they demanded. So Moses cried out to the Lord for help, and the Lord showed him a branch. Moses took the branch and threw it into the water. This made the water good to drink. It was there at Marah that the Lord laid before them the following conditions to test their faithfulness to him.' (Exodus 15:25)

They were complaining and blaming despite their miraculous delivery from Egypt.

In Psalm 137 we see the children of Israel in exile in Babylon, angry, seeking revenge and refusing to praise and worship.

'By the rivers of Babylon we sat and wept when we remembered Zion.

There on the poplars we hung our harps, for there our captors asked us for songs, our tormentors demanded songs of joy; they said, "Sing us one of the songs of Zion!"

How can we sing the songs of the LORD while in a foreign land? If I forget you, Jerusalem, may my right hand forget its skill. May my tongue cling to the roof of my mouth if I do not remember you, if I do not consider Jerusalem my highest joy.

Remember, LORD, what the Edomites did on the day Jerusalem fell. "Tear it down," they cried, "tear it down to its foundations!" Daughterof Babylon, doomed to destruction, happy is the one who repays you according to what you have done to us. Happy is the one who seizes

172

your infants and dashes them against the rocks.' (Psalm 137 NIV)

The Edomites were blood brothers who didn't come to the rescue of the Jews. They rejoiced in the Israelites defeat, the ultimate betrayal. It's hard to read in the light of the revelation of Christ, but maybe in our brokenness, vulnerability, bitterness and anger we have feelings of revenge and hatred?

In the story of Jonah we see how Jonah was stuck in how he thought God should treat the Ninevites and himself. He did not want them to repent. However, God saw that they had turned away from their evil lives and changed His mind about them. What He said He would do to them He didn't do.

`*Jonah was furious. He lost his temper. He yelled at God, "God! I knew it - when I was back home, I knew this was going to happen! That's why I ran off to Tarshish! I knew you were sheer grace and mercy, not easily angered, rich in love, and ready at the drop of a hat to turn your plans of punishment into a programme of forgiveness!*

So, God, if you won't kill them, kill me! I'm better off dead!" God said, "What do you have to be angry about?"

But Jonah just left. He went out of the city to the east and sat down in a sulk. He put together a makeshift shelter of leafy branches and sat there in the shade to see what would happen to the city.

God arranged for a broad-leafed tree to spring up. It grew over Jonah to cool him off and get him out of his angry sulk. Jonah was pleased and enjoyed the shade. Life was looking up.

But then God sent a worm. By dawn of the next day, the worm had bored into the shade tree and it withered away. The sun came up and God sent a hot, blistering wind from the east. The sun beat down on Jonah's head and he started to faint. He prayed to die: "I'm better off dead!"

Then God said to Jonah, "What right do you have to get angry about this shade tree?" Jonah said, "Plenty of right. It's made me angry enough to die!"

God said, "What's this? How is it that you can change your feelings from pleasure to anger overnight about a mere shade tree that you did nothing to get? You neither planted nor watered it. It grew up one night and died the next night. So, why can't I likewise change what I feel about Nineveh from anger to pleasure, this big city of more than a hundred and twenty thousand childlike people who don't yet know right from wrong, to say nothing of all the innocent animals?" (Jonah 4 - The Message)

C S Lewis said, 'God will use all repented evil as fuel for fresh good in the end.' [50] But we struggle with this especially when God applies it to others, like Jonah. Jonah was happy when God saved him from the fish but not when the Ninevites were saved. He was more concerned about his reputation because now none of his warnings would come true. We want judgement and destruction for those people or things we decide or know are evil. Jonah condemns God based on his own judgement of what is just and consistent. He does not want God to be who God is: - just, merciful and compassionate, slow to anger and responsive to people's repentance.

God chose Jonah for a difficult task: prophesying not to his own people, Israel, but to the enemy. The Ninevites, residents of the capital of the Assyrian Empire, were idolatrous and known for heinous acts of violence and cruelty. They were also the people God had said would later overtake Israel. Considering Nineveh's reputation and its relationship to Israel, it's no wonder Jonah struggled with God's command to go and preach judgement.

Jonah felt reluctant to follow God's command. It was not that Jonah was afraid to enter Nineveh (although that would have been reasonable) - it was because he knew God too well. He knew God to be '*a gracious God and merciful, slow to anger, and abounding in steadfast love, and ready to relent from punishing.*' (Jonah 4:2 NRSV) If the Ninevites should repent, Jonah reasoned, God would forgive. This was not acceptable to Jonah and it made him angry.

Jonah may have possessed a keen understanding of God's mercy on one level, but at a deeper level he didn't understand holy mercy at all. Indeed, Jonah himself experienced this same mercy after running from God and his implausible task, and being thrown into the sea. "*As my life was ebbing away,*" he prayed inside the fish, "*I remembered the Lord; and my prayer came to you...Deliverance belongs to the Lord!*" (2:7,9) Jonah could thank God for the mercy he received. He could expect mercy towards Israel, which also had proven idolatrous and periodically cruel. Yet he could not tolerate God's mercy offered to the other side, the enemy. Had he really understood the stunning depth of God's mercy, Jonah would have shared God's love even for the vile Ninevites. We can decide how God should respond and remain stuck, or we can choose to respond differently.

A man who lived long after Jonah received a call from God to go to a people similarly idolatrous and cruel. His story resembles Jonah's in many ways, but unlike Jonah, he came to understand God's mercy and share God's love for the enemy. Patrick was captured at age sixteen by a band of Celtic pirates and taken from his home in England to Ireland, where he was sold into slavery. A nominal Christian, Patrick experienced a great deepening in his with-God life during six years of captivity. In living with his captors he came to understand the Celtic people, learning their language and experiencing their culture. He grew to love them.

One night, in a dream, Patrick heard a voice telling him a ship was ready to take him home. The next day he escaped to the coast, boarded a ship, and made it back to England. Patrick served the Church until the age of forty-eight, when he had another dream that changed the course of his life. In it, an angel read a letter from his former Irish captors, who cried, 'We appeal to you, holy servant boy, to come and walk among us.' Interpreting the dream as God's call for him to return voluntarily to the Celtic peoples of Ireland, Patrick launched an Irish Christian movement, baptizing tens of thousands of people and planting hundreds of churches. His evangelistic approach grew even more successful in the generations following his death.

Unlike Jonah, captivity fostered in Patrick God-shaped mercy for all people, even his enemies. We can choose to be like Jonah, stingy without grace and generous with our judgements or we can recall God's lavish forgiveness and love, keeping his mercy ever before us as our guide. [51]

Prayer for the Right Attitude

Father, again I ask for the right balance in my 'how things should be' thinking. Help me to understand, as I release my anger and resentment, that I'm not compromising or accepting lower standards but I am rather learning to love in a broken world.

I ask for the grace and healing to use what has happened to me in a way that makes me more like St Patrick than Jonah. Help me to stop clinging to past sufferings and adding those sufferings to my present pain. Help me to refuse self-pity and instead, turn my eyes to You.

Please speak to me as you did to Hagar (Genesis 16:11) and tell me you have heard my woes, so that I may be able to say, '*You are the God who sees.*' (Genesis 16:13) Amen

Ask the Questions

Many of the Psalms portrays stark words of anguish, for instance Psalm 77:7-10 (NIV)

`Will the Lord reject forever? Will he never show his favour again? Has his unfailing love vanished forever? Has his promise failed for all time?

Has God forgotten to be merciful? Has he in anger withheld his compassion?

Then I thought, "To this I will appeal: the years when the Most High stretched out his right hand."'

Nevertheless the songwriter goes on to recall and meditate on God's dramatic victory. In the midst of our suffering and questions, we too can call to mind what God has done for us in the past.

`I will remember the deeds of the LORD; yes, I will remember your miracles of long ago. I will consider all your works and meditate on all your mighty deeds.

181

Your ways, God, are holy. What god is as great as our God? You are the God who performs miracles; you display your power among the peoples.
With your mighty arm you redeemed your people, the descendants of Jacob and Joseph.

The waters saw you, God, the waters saw you and writhed; the very depths were convulsed. The clouds poured down water, the heavens resounded with thunder; your arrows flashed back and forth. Your thunder was heard in the whirlwind, your lightning lit up the world; the earth trembled and quaked.

Your path led through the sea, your way through the mighty waters, though your footprints were not seen. You led your people like a flock by the hand of Moses and Aaron.' (Psalm 77:11-20 NIV)

Further on in the Bible we read Jeremiah's questions.

'You are always righteous, Lord, when I bring a case before you.

Yet I would speak with you about your justice: Why does

the way of the wicked prosper? Why do all the faithless

live at ease? You have planted them, and they have taken

root; they grow and bear fruit. You are always on their

lips but far from their hearts. Yet you know me, LORD; you

see me and test my thoughts about you.

Drag them off like sheep to be butchered! Set them apart

for the day of slaughter!

How long will the land lie parched and the grass in every

field be withered?

Because those who live in it are wicked, the animals and

birds have perished.

Moreover, the people are saying, "He will not see what

happens to us."' (Jeremiah 12:1-4 NIV)

Jeremiah was worn down by opposition, absorbed with self-pity and complaining. But he was facing God and asking, even though he knew God was right. Asking questions is permissible. John the Baptist, about whom I wrote earlier in the chapter, when in prison doubted if Jesus really was the Son of God, so he sent his disciples to ask.

'Are you the one who is to come, or should we expect someone else?' (Matthew 11:2-3)

Jesus on the cross asks THE question, "*My God, my God why have you forsaken me?*"

Lots of us have questions that continually circulate in our minds demanding an answer. We need to learn to turn them outward to God. Such questions as:-

Why me?

Can I really get better?

Why did you make me like this?

God, can you be trusted?

Where were you God, when it happened?

Are your promises true?

Did you, Father God, not promise to protect us? Be with us? Provide for us?

Are you always in control?

Why did you let this happen?

Orual, in C S Lewis's novel, 'Till We Have Faces', isolates herself, hiding behind a wall because she is ugly. This has caused her much suffering, so she builds her case against the gods. The first part of the book, among other things, is the story of the list of her complaints. When she challenges the gods, she receives no answers and experiences only separateness.

Finally she is brought to the side of a pool, where she comes to know the presence of God, and is pierced through with joy and sweetness, dispelling the despair and bitterness. And she, the fiercely ugly one, is made new. When she looks into the water she is clothed and beautiful. She hears the Voice calling her by her new name and says, 'I ended my book with the words "No answer". I know now why you utter "No answer" - You, Yourself, are the answer!'

Brother Francis, a children's palliative care nurse says, 'Suffering is not a question that demands an answer: it is not a problem that demands a solution: it is a mystery that demands a

Presence." [52]

Ask the Question

Father God, you know these questions go round and round in my head. And I realise because of my anger, bitterness and insistence on an answer that I am tempted to feel justified in my desire to continue thinking like this. Please help me.

It can be helpful at this point to picture your question or questions as a solid question mark. Then using your hand choose to take the question mark(s) from your mind or heart and put them on the cross of Jesus.

Father, I now ask you in that place outside of our time where all time is present to you, to absorb my question(s) into Jesus' great question which encapsulates so much of my pain, *'My God, my God why have you forsaken me.'*

And I ask Father God, that like Job I will be able to say - *'I know that you can do anything, and no one can stop you. You asked, "Who is this that questions my wisdom with such ignorance"? It is I—and I was talking about things I knew nothing about, things far too wonderful for me.'* (Job 42:1-3)

Amen

Responding positively

As I have already written, life is difficult and often it is not fair. Our experience of suffering follows neither strict standards of rationality nor clear patterns of predictability. Suffering does not respect the boundaries of right or wrong, innocence or guilt, deserved or undeserved. More often than not, one person sins and another person suffers the consequences.

Alexander Solzhenitsyn said, 'If only there were evil people somewhere committing evil deeds and it was necessary only to separate them from the rest of us and destroy them. But the line dividing good and evil cuts through the heart of every human being. And who is willing to destroy a piece of his own heart'? [53]

One of the keys to the answer of the question 'How will I suffer?' is to think, To whom will I go. We can isolate, blame, become bitter and resent how things are or in our fear, pain and confusion we can turn to Jesus.

John 6:68 - 'To whom else shall I go? You alone have the words of eternal life.'

Dallas Willard says, 'Basic human freedom depends on where you put your mind.'[54]

During World War II, Viktor Frankl, a Jewish psychiatrist and a concentration camp survivor, lost nearly everything including his wife. Suffering was imposed on him. Frankl observed that most prisoners in the camps allowed their circumstances to control their lives but this was not true for everyone. Amazingly some decided to exercise the power of choice.

'Even though conditions such as lack of sleep, insufficient food and various mental stresses may suggest that the inmates were bound to react in certain ways, in the final analysis it becomes clear that the sort of person the prisoner became was the result of an inner decision, and not the result of camp influences alone. Fundamentally, therefore, any man can, even under such circumstances, decide what should become of him -

mentally and spiritually. He may retain his human dignity even in a concentration camp.' [55]

Frankl concluded, 'Everything can be taken away from us save one thing - our choice of attitude to the situation.'

We always have the power to choose. Another answer to the question - 'How will I suffer'? is with further 'how' questions. In the midst of suffering we can ask Jesus, 'How can I love today?', 'How do I pray today?', 'How can I practise your presence today?'

Martin Luther King said, 'The ultimate nature of man is not where he stands in moments of comfort but where he stands in times of challenge and controversy.'[56]

Genesis 50:20 says, '*That which you intended for evil, God has used for good.*'

My son Dominic, when he was a toddler, each night in bed examined every 'wound' and mark! We can do something similar, and do it with resentment, anger and bitterness or we can look to God and show Him our wounds or suffering.

Mary and Martha are good examples of people who went to Jesus in their loss, pain, confusion and suffering. We see in John 11 that Jesus not only doesn't punish them for being real, but goes with them - and us - to the depths of grief. Mary and Martha send word to Jesus about their brother Lazarus: '*Lord, he who you love is ill.*' (v3) Jesus deliberately stays where he is for two days, and Lazarus dies. By the time Jesus approaches Bethany Lazarus has already been dead four days.

Martha goes out to meet Jesus, while Mary stays back, grieving in the house. '*Lord, if you had been here, my brother would not have died. But even now I know that God will give whatever you ask him.*' (v21)

Martha's complaint is strong and so is her faith. Yet in the ensuing conversation it is clear that she has no expectation that Jesus can or will resurrect her brother before the last day. Jesus responds, '*I am the resurrection and the life. Whoever believes in me shall never die,*'(v 25) and invites her to believe - in him. Her affirmation of faith in the aftermath of Lazarus's premature death, that he is Christ, Son of God, the Coming One energises her as she stands before him.

Mary came where Jesus was and saw him; she knelt at his feet and repeated Martha's exact complaint but without Martha's confession of faith: '*Lord, if you had been here, my brother would not have died.*'(v32)

Jesus is deeply impacted. He doesn't correct her, explain himself or in any way justify his absence. A series of verbs shows Jesus' increasing closeness to Mary, Martha, and their dead brother. When he sees her weeping, and the Jews who came with her also weeping, and he is '*greatly disturbed in spirit and deeply moved.*'(v33)

Jesus shows God's willingness to go with us fully into our pain. Rather than distancing himself through theological reflection, Jesus asks: '*Where have you laid him*'? (v34) The people invite him deeper into the concrete details of their upset: '*Come and see,*' - and Jesus weeps.

Jesus' empathy leads some in the crowd to complain as we sometimes do: '*Could not he who opened the eyes of the blind man have kept this man from dying*? (v37). The crowd doesn't complain directly to Jesus as Martha and Mary do, but talk about him in the third person.

Regardless of different people's ways of addressing Jesus, the text says nothing to criticise people or to justify Jesus. Rather Jesus shows a willingness to go even deeper into people's root disappointments and loss. How far will Jesus go? Much further than we will it seems. [57]

I first discovered the truth of Christ's deep involvement in our suffering through a dream. The beginning of the dream was a picture of a white screen with the words set out like this –

C

H

R

I

S

T

CRIES WITH US

It then became

CHRIST

Comforter

Risen One

Intercessor

Eternal

Saviour

WITH US

I woke and in my daily reading, which was a reflection by Eugene Peterson on Psalm 6, I read: -

'Tears are a biological gift of God. They are a physical means for expressing emotional and spiritual experience. But it is hard to know what to do with them. If we indulge our tears we cultivate self-pity. If we suppress our tears we lose touch with our feelings. But if we pray our tears we enter into............... that integrate our sorrows with our Lord's sorrows and discover both the source of and relief from our sadness.'[58]

'I am worn out from my groaning. All night long I flood my bed with weeping and drench my couch with tears. My eyes grow weak with sorrow; they fail because of all my foes.' (Psalm 6:6-7 NIV)

'Those who plant in tears will harvest in shouts of joy. They weep as they go to plant their seed, but they sing as they return with the harvest.' (Psalm 126:5-6)

I see your tears

Those you shed and those you swallow

I am with you in your pain.

Those tears you give to me, I can transform

I see them like the dew on a bud glistening in the morning light –

I see them softening the ground - melting the rocks.

As the light of My love shines through them, they radiate like diamonds.

Pray that you may see as I see –

The sunshine of My love mingled with your tears, causes My rainbows
of promises to be blazoned across the sky.

Look through your tears with eyes of faith.

See the prisms of My lights dawning on the horizon.

Believe in what is yet to be.

Lin Button

Prayer for Comfort

Father of all mercy, God of all comfort, please come and be with me as I go through hard times. And in Your time I ask I will also be there for someone else in their time of need. I ask for your healing comfort and help to trust in You totally.

Thank you that real joy and peace is not dependent on my circumstances, but your presence. Be very real to me, I pray. Amen

The truth of Job 42:2 is illustrated well in the following story.

The Tale of Three Trees

Once upon a mountain top, three little trees stood and dreamed of what they wanted to become when they grew up. The first little tree looked up at the stars and said: "I want to hold treasure. I want to be covered with gold and filled with precious stones. I'll be the most beautiful treasure chest in the world!" The second little tree looked out at the small stream trickling by on its way to the ocean. "I want to be traveling mighty waters and carrying powerful kings. I'll be the strongest ship in the world!" The third little tree looked down into the valley below where busy men and women worked in a busy town. "I don't want to leave the mountain top at all. I want to grow so tall that when people stop to look at me, they'll raise their eyes to heaven and think of God. I will be the tallest tree in the world."

Years passed and the little trees grew tall. One day three woodcutters climbed the mountain. The first woodcutter looked at the first tree and said, "This tree is beautiful. It is perfect for me." With a swoop of his shining ax, the first tree fell. "Now I shall be made into a beautiful chest, I shall hold wonderful treasure!" the first tree said. The second woodcutter looked at the second tree and said, "This tree is strong. It is perfect for me." With a swoop of his shining ax, the second tree fell. "Now I shall sail mighty waters!" thought the second tree. "I shall be a strong ship for mighty kings!" The third tree felt her heart sink when the last woodcutter looked her way. She stood straight and tall and pointed bravely to heaven. But the woodcutter

198

never even looked up. "Any kind of tree will do for me." He muttered. With a swoop of his shining ax the third tree fell.

The first tree rejoiced when the woodcutter brought her to a carpenter's shop. But the carpenter fashioned the tree into a feed box for animals. The once beautiful tree was not covered with gold, nor with treasure. She was coated with sawdust and filled with hay for hungry farm animals. The second tree smiled when the woodcutter took her to a shipyard, but no mighty ship was made that day. Instead, the once strong tree was hammered and sawed into a simple fishing boat. She was too small and too weak to sail to an ocean, or even a river. Instead she was taken to a little lake. The third tree was confused when the woodcutter cut her into strong beams and left her in a lumberyard. "What happened?" The once tall tree wondered. "All I ever wanted was to stay on the mountain top and point to God..."

Many, many days and nights passed. The three trees nearly forgot their dreams. But one night, golden starlight poured over the first tree as a young woman placed her newborn baby in the feed box. "I wish I could make a cradle for him," her husband whispered. The mother squeezed his hand and smiled as the starlight shone on the smooth and the sturdy wood. "This manger is beautiful," she said. And suddenly the first tree knew he was holding the greatest treasure in the world.

One evening a tired traveler and his friends crowded into the old fishing boat. The traveler fell asleep as the second tree quietly sailed out into the lake. Soon a thundering and thrashing storm arose. The little tree shuddered. She knew she did not have the strength to carry so many passengers safely through the wind and the

rain. The tired man awakened. He stood up, stretched out
his hand and said, "Peace." The storm stopped as quickly
as it had begun. And suddenly the second tree knew he
was carrying the King of heaven and earth.

One Friday morning, the third tree was startled when her
beams were yanked from the forgotten woodpile. She flinched
as she was carried through an angry jeering crowd. She
shuddered when soldiers nailed a man's hands to her. She felt
ugly and harsh and cruel. But on Sunday morning, when the
sun rose and the earth trembled with joy beneath her, the third
tree knew that God's love had changed everything. It had
made the third tree strong. And every time people thought of
the third tree, they would think of God. That was better than
being the tallest tree in the world. So the next time you feel
down because you didn't get what you want, just sit tight and be
happy because God is thinking of something better to give you.

5

Confession is a gift that we need to unwrap. Shame stops us: 'I am not worthy.' Pride stops us: 'I do not need it', though I would suggest that pride can be a symptom, a barrier to accessing the painful feelings of shame. Pretending and hiding stops us, as well as disappointment and a resentful attitude to suffering. They are all barriers to receiving the gift of confession.

This gift is much like knowing a dentist is a gift if we have toothache.

The writers of the Psalms were very clear in their hostility towards sinners. The Psalmists wanted them to suffer in a way that is often shocking to our modern ears. They did not separate the sin from the sinner in the way that God looks at sin. Yet something of their intolerance towards sin, their refusal to condone or rationalize, in fact, their outright hostility to sin reflects something of God's divine voice. As C. S. Lewis writes: -

'That tooth must come out, that right hand must be
amputated, if the man is to be saved. In that way the
restlessness of the Psalmists is far nearer to one side of
the truth than many modern attitudes which can be
mistaken, by those who hold them, for Christian
charity.'[59]

As I wrote in chapter 2, another of our difficulties in seeing
confession as a gift is the false belief that admitting to any
wrongdoing will make us feel worse. There is a story Tony
Campolo tells of praying with a prostitute who was crying. When
he had finished praying he said, 'Why don't you go to church on
Sunday'?, to which she replied, 'Why would I do that? Don't you
think I feel bad enough as it is?'[60] Yet we need to confess when
we have done something wrong or have neglected to love
others. One of the Anglican Prayer Book confession prayers is: -

Almighty God, our heavenly Father,

We have sinned against you and against our fellow men,

In thought and word and deed,

Through negligence, through weakness,

Through our own deliberate fault.

We are truly sorry

And repent of all our sins.

For the sake of your Son Jesus Christ, who died for us,

Forgive us all that is past;

And grant that we may serve you in newness of life;

To the glory of your Name. Amen

The underlying perspective is that God is holy and yet, despite our sin and uncleanness, He seeks to be with us, to give life and experience relationship with us. He understands that we fracture relationship with Him, others, and ourselves through our sin, but our confession and Jesus' death for us provide a way for us to be forgiven, cleansed and healed. God thus continues to be present to us to bless us.

Therefore Jesus on the cross, becoming a sin-offering for us, enables us to experience life-giving, restored relationship. The Catholic church near where I live reflects this well, describing confession as the sacrament of reconciliation. The

Scriptures contain many verses encouraging us to receive this gift.

Leviticus 5:5 *'When any of the people become aware of their guilt in any of these ways they must confess their sins.'*

Psalm 32:5 *'Finally I confessed all my sins to you and stopped trying to hide them. I said to myself 'I will confess my rebellion to the Lord.' And you forgave me! All my guilt is gone.'*

Psalm 38:18 *'I confess my iniquity. I am sorry for my sin.'*

Psalm 66:1 *'If I had not confessed the sin in my heart my Lord would not have listened.'*

Isaiah 1:18 *'"Come now, let us argue this out. says the Lord." "No matter how deep the stains of your sins I can remove it. I can make you as clear as fresh fallen snow. Even if you are stained as red as crimson I can make you white as wool.'"*

Matthew 3:6 *'They were baptized by Him in the River Jordan confessing their sins.'*

1 John 1:9 *'If we confess our sin, God is faithful and just to forgive our sins and cleanse us from all unrighteousness.'*

James 5:16 *'Confess your sins to one another that you may be healed.'*

How do we know we have sinned? There is such a thing as 'healthy guilt'. Mark Twain says, 'Man is the only animal that blushes.'[61] Pain is the language of the body that alerts us to when something needs attention and in the same way, guilt forces us to give attention to something we would prefer to ignore or cover up. It creates an inner battle when we believe one way and act another. Ultimately the guilt; ideally so disturbs us that we take the difficult step of confessing.

A word of warning: we need to listen to God concerning our sin as we cannot always rely on our conscience. A mature, healthy conscience is biblically trained with a Holy Spirit monitor. A very broken conscience registers little or no guilt (like a leper not registering physical pain leading to an permanent damage). A wounded or immature conscience may be immature, punitive, self- condemning, and give rise to false guilt.

We can be very prone to negative, condemning 'self-talk' leading to false guilt and false shame. False guilt can cause psychological dysfunction and physical and mental ill-health.

FALSE GUILT

It is said that, if you put fleas in a jar they jump out: put them in a jar with a lid on and they jump up, hit the lid, and continue to do this for some time. If you then remove the lid, they will still only jump as high as the lid and land back in the glass jar! We can behave in a similar way, yet we are supposed to be free. Feelings of guilt and condemnation are like an invisible lid that we hit our head against when we attempt to move into freedom. What is confusing is that the lid does exist: when we are truly guilty; 'hitting our head' against the holy law of God gives us a revelation concerning our guilt before Him. The law is holy, showing us that we are not, and that is partly what it is meant to do. Much like pain, it is a gift, i.e. touch something hot and pain tells us to let go. Without pain we could really damage ourselves, but pain that goes on and on when there is no danger is not a gift.[62]

Just as our physical bodies speak loudly through pain so that we will attend to the injury, our consciences speak in the language of guilt so that we will take the steps necessary for healing. The goal in both is to restore health, not to feel bad. When we feel a twinge of conscience, we should first ask whether we've done something deserving true guilt. In other words, have we really sinned? If the answer is yes, then we dare not avoid or repress that guilt. Like pain, it warns of something that endangers our health.

Guilt that goes on and on, even after repentance and receiving God's forgiveness, is not a gift, it is a spiritual disease. Guilt of this nature is false. It torments us keeping us down and we live like fleas in a lidless jar, only jumping as high as our flea mentality! Once I was confessing a sin all day, asking why I received no assurance of forgiveness. God said, 'You haven't sinned!'

We may struggle with trying to be good enough for God, judging ourselves by our internal 'measuring sticks', or we may suffer from obsession or introspection. A mixture of unrealistic expectation combined with a spiritualizing form of perfectionism can cause obsessive self-examination such as Martin Luther experienced in his first years as a monk. He would exhaust his confessors with his introspection and unhealthy thoughts. 'To diagnose smallpox you do not have to probe each pustule, nor do you heal each separately.'[63]

False guilt is a state we may cultivate or a mood we may slip into for a few days. Healthy guilt has a directional movement, first pointing backward to the sin and then pointing forward to change. A person who feels no guilt can never find healing, yet neither can a person who wallows in guilt. The sense of guilt only serves its designated purpose as a symptom if it presses us toward healing.

HEALTHY CONFESSION

So what does healthy confession look like? 'Repentance is not something God demands of you before he will take you back, writes C. S. Lewis in *Mere Christianity*. 'It is simply a description of what going back is like. It opens the way to the future, relationship restored, another step on the way.'[64]

The bible encourages us in many different ways.

'*Return to the Lord your God with all your heart*'. Jeremiah 4 encourages us to return to God.

We read '*For Christ Jesus, who knew no sin, became our sin, so that by His death we are released from sin, and in His resurrection we "become the righteousness of God."* 2 Corinthians 5:21 NRSV

Since God has now reconciled the world to Himself in Christ we can celebrate the truth. '*Behold, now is the day of salvation*'. 2 Corinthians 6:2 NRSV

'*He calls us to return to Him with all our heart because He is gracious and merciful, slow to anger, abounding in steadfast love and relents from punishing*'. Joel 2: 13 NRSV

So we can approach our Father in faith and confidence trusting all that Christ has done for us.

In the story of the woman caught in adultery, Jesus, in a brilliant stroke of genius says, '*Let him who is without sin throw the first stone'* and thereby replaces the righteous and the guilty with two different categories - sinners who admit and sinners who deny.

Admitting our guilt enables us to be forgiven. The accusers having denied any sin walked away hidden in their robes of respectability and received nothing.

It is interesting to note the Bible always refers to her as '*the woman caught in adultery'* (John 8:3) not as an adulteress. The act is described as sin but she is not named by it and shamed.

Forgiveness needs to be accepted as well as offered if it is to be complete. A man who admits no guilt can accept no forgiveness. For instance, a woman's husband had an affair. His wife has forgiven him, but he has never accepted any responsibility therefore there was no true reconciliation or completeness.

Leanne Payne says there are three barriers to healing, as follows:

- Failure to confess our sins and to receive forgiveness

- Failure to forgive others

- Failure to accept ourselves

Expressing this in different language, the steps I lead people through are:

- Listening to God for ourselves

- Receiving forgiveness

- Acknowledging the wounds and sins against us

- Forgiving those who sin against us

- Confessing our sinful responses

- Receiving forgiveness

- Looking at the lies that the wounds and sin have caused us to believe about God and ourselves

- The gift and discipline of Self-acceptance

There is an obvious link between sin and healing. I am not saying that everyone who is sick or who has not been healed is stuck in some kind of sin. However, in 'The Principles of Internal Medicine' (Harrison) it was reported that 50-80% of all physical disorders have psychosomatic or stress-related origins.

'Psychosomatic' does not mean that it is imagined, rather it means that emotional pain or sin is affecting us physically. As we have seen, false guilt can damage us. True guilt needs to be confessed and forgiveness received. Jesus died for our guilt as well as for our sin. Guilt saps our energy. We all have the capacity to choose whether or not to sin; to turn towards fulfillment or nothingness, towards life or death. In sin we turn towards nothingness, the old nature, the false self.

Every time we sin we are turning towards death, away from life, away from 'becoming'. We are choosing 'non-being'. Choosing not to sin means turning towards the grace-filled union, '*Christ within, the hope of glory*', (Colossians 1:27) towards grace, the empowering presence of God within, without, above. The yoke of sin binds us to our nothingness. More deeply than is comfortable for us to think, we are all in rebellion to God!

DEFINITION OF SIN

'Sin is always a departure from the norm and is assessed accordingly. Sin is deviant and perverse, an INjustice or INiquity or INgratitude. Sin in the Exodus literature is DISorder and DISobedience. Sin is faithlessness, lawlessness, godlessness. Sin is both the overstepping of a line and the failure to reach it - both transgression and shortcoming. Sin is a missing of the mark, a spoiling of goods, a staining of garments, a hitch in one's gait, a wandering from the path, a fragmentation of the whole. Sin is what culpably DISTURBS normal shalom. Sinful human life is a caricature of proper human life. So the biggest biblical idea about sin, expressed in a riot of images and terms is that sin is an anomaly, an intruder, a notorious gatecrasher. Sin does not belong in God's world.'

Cornelius Plantinga Jnr goes on to write, 'Sin is also a parasite, an uninvited guest that keeps tapping its host for sustenance. Nothing about sin is its own; all its power,

213

persistence and plausibility are stolen goods. Sin is not really an entity but a spoiler of entities, not an organism but a leech on organisms. Sin does not build shalom; it vandalizes it. In metaphysical perspective, evil offers no true alternative to good, as if the two were equal and opposite qualities.'[65]

'Goodness', says C. S. Lewis, 'is, so to speak, itself: badness is only spoiled goodness. And there must be something good first before it can be spoiled.'[66]

Here Lewis reproduces the old Augustinian idea that evil has no existence except as a privation of good. Good is original, independent and constructive; evil is derivative, dependent and destructive. To be successful, evil needs what it hijacks from goodness.

IS ALL SIN THE SAME?

James 2: 10 *'For any person who keeps all the laws except one is as guilty as the person who has broken all of God's laws.'*

All sin is equally wrong but not all sin is equally bad. Some good acts are better than others and some wrong acts worse than others.

Consider the Second Helvetic Confession:[67] which says that we confess that sins are not equal; although they arise from the same fountain of corruption and unbelief, some are more serious than others. As the Lord said, '*It will be more tolerable for Sodom than for the city that rejects the word of the gospel.*' (Matthew 10:15, 11:20-24)

Behind the James verse is the idea that you can't break the law a little bit. Failure to jump over the river means we got wet whether we miss the other bank by three yards or one foot. This truth is intended to lead us to repentance not feelings of hopelessness and despair.

Jesus said that contemplating going over it in our minds is as bad as doing it.

(Matthew 5: 27-28) '*You have heard that it was said, "You shall not commit adultery." But I tell you that anyone who looks at a woman lustfully has already committed adultery with her in his heart.'*

If we think all sin is the same and thinking about things is as bad as doing then we feel, 'I may as well give up', tormented and damned. Christians know that adultery in one's heart damages others less than if enacted in a hotel room and therefore ranks as less serious. However, nursed, sinful thoughts in our hearts and imaginations are subtle and progressive, often having more effects on our relationships than we realise.[68]

Under the weight of this realization, it would be easy to give up or to decline into feeling continually bad. But that is not God's intention. God is good, wise and loving. He knows what we are up against and has made provision for us. If we limit our understanding to the 'all sin is the same' concept, we miss God's heart.

In the Bible there are different aspects to sin. For instance, there is that which is usually translated as 'iniquity' meaning weakness, the tendency to fall under temptation in specific areas, our particular area of vulnerability towards, an "Achilles heel", bent towards a sinful pattern. This is the word used in Exodus 20:5

'You shall not bow down to them nor serve them. For I, the Lord your God, am a jealous God, visiting the iniquity of the fathers upon the children to the third and fourth generations of those who hate Me.' (NKJV)

We all have 'bents' or vulnerabilities in certain areas but we don't have to act on them. This can be seen in all sorts of areas such as alcoholism, which affects families from generation to generation. By confession God can heal.

Another aspect is transgression. This is more than 'bent'; it is the willful action to cross the line. It suggests more of a deliberate action of wrongdoing. We are not to identify with, excuse or embrace it: we need to confess it. The same applies where there has been a defection, rebellion, or an entering into a covenant with darkness.

One memory I have of the word 'sin', before I was a Christian, came from having once seen a sign over the door of a small mission hall: '*Enter Here All Ye Sinners.*' However, my concept of sin before I was a Christian meant that in my own mind, I wasn't a sinner! I hadn't committed adultery, murdered or burgled anyone, and the things I did that maybe could do with some improvement - like drinking, smoking or swearing - weren't really sins: everyone did them, well everyone I knew! But now I realize that, as a Christian, it isn't just a matter of a stray sin here or there, but patterns in our hearts that need confessing and healing.

PATTERNS OF THE HEART

These can be such things as: -

- Internal negative judgement of others or self

- Disapproving of others

- Inability to be generous

- Deceit: How many of us would ring a credit card company who had made a mistake in our favour? What if we are given too much change at the checkout?

- False insurance claims

- Withholding information that might incriminate us

- Blaming someone else

- Permanent discontent: never being satisfied, always wanting that bit more, a bit more excitement, money, love, attention or approval

- Addictions: who is the master? Drinking too much, relying on food or drink as a comfort

- Living beyond our means: could you afford to pay off your credit cards?

- Withdrawing: not speaking to someone who has hurt us, withholding love

- Activism: too busy in order to avoid intimacy with God and others

- Self protection: fear of making mistakes, self-preservation, hiding

- Comparing ourselves to others, judging others, competing with others

So often our sin seems more powerful as our desire to stop. Philip Yancey writes of this in '*Rumours of Another World,*' and quotes from *Moby Dick* by Herman Melville:

'What is it, what nameless, inscrutable, unearthly thing is it; what cozzening, hidden lord and master, and cruel, remorseless emperor commands me; that against all natural lovings and longings, I so keep pushing, and crowding, and jamming myself on all the time; recklessly making me ready to do what in my own proper, natural heart, I durst not so much as dare'? [69]

Captain Ahab, the obsessed hunter of Moby Dick is speaking about the great white whale. Ahab ignores dreadful warnings against his fateful mission; his crew's pleas to abandon the chase fall on deaf ears; he even coldly refuses to search for another captain's lost son in order to continue his quest. He cannot control himself. The whale, 'all a magnet', has Ahab in its mighty field of force. The First mate, Starbuck, sees to the heart of the matter, crying out to Ahab, 'Desist. See! Moby Dick seeks thee not. It is thou, thou, that madly seekest him!' Here Philip Yancey then writes: -

' Here lies the inscrutable power of evil. I can calmly identify my own sins and affirm how much better my life would be if rid of them. Yet knowing that I should choose the good, even willing that I should, does not make me choose the good. Like Captain Ahab, yes, like Bill Clinton, (or other fallen church leaders or prophets) sometimes I feel caught in a force field I can neither explain nor resist.'[70]

'"There remains in the regenerate a smouldering cinder of evil, from which desires continually leap forth to allure and spur to commit sin," said John Calvin.[71]

"If only evil did resemble a smouldering cinder that we could locate and stomp out. Instead, we more resemble tiny magnets, with one end attracted to and the other end repelled by the same force. Cut a magnet in half and you get a smaller magnet with the same polarity.

Cut it again, and again, into sixteen pieces and you have

sixteen pieces attracted on one end and repelled on the

other. In just that way the tendency to yield to evil and

also to resist it infuses every part of my body, as a kind of

inbuilt cellular tension.'"[72]

Long before I read this I would often, when praying for

people, see magnets and I would pray, 'Switch the magnets'. I

would see them as having magnetized brain cells which, despite

the person's desire to change, were attracted to the wrong force

(addiction etc). I would pray, 'Switch them so they are repelled

by the force and attracted towards facing the throne room of

God.' This is very much like St Paul's letter to the Romans within

chapters 7 and 8 (The Message).

7:17 'But I need something more! For if I know the

law but still can't keep it, and if the power of sin within

me keeps sabotaging my best intentions, I obviously need

help! I realize that I don't have what it takes. I can will it,

but I can't do it. I decide to do good, but I don't really do it; I decide not to do bad, but then I do it anyway. My decisions, such as they are, don't result in actions. Something has gone wrong deep within me and gets the better of me every time. It happens so regularly that it's predictable. The moment I decide to do good, sin is there to trip me up. I truly delight in God's commands, but it's pretty obvious that not all of me joins in that delight. Parts of me covertly rebel, and just when I least expect it, they take charge.

I've tried everything and nothing helps. I'm at the end of my rope. Is there no one who can do anything for me? Isn't that the real question?

The answer, thank God, is that Jesus Christ can and does. He acted to set things right in this life of contradictions where I want to serve God with all my heart and mind, but am pulled by the influence of sin to do something totally different.

Chapter 8: With the arrival of Jesus, the Messiah, that fateful dilemma is resolved. Those who enter into Christ's being-here-for-us no longer have to live under a continuous, low-lying black cloud. A new power is in operation. The Spirit of life in Christ, like a strong wind, has magnificently cleared the air, freeing you from a fated lifetime of brutal tyranny at the hands of sin and death.

God went for the jugular when he sent his own Son. He didn't deal with the problem as something remote and unimportant. In his Son, Jesus, he personally took on the human condition, entered the disordered mess of struggling humanity in order to set it right once and for all. The law code, weakened as it always was by fractured human nature, could never have done that.

The law always ended up being used as a Band-Aid on sin instead of a deep healing of it. And now what the law code asked for but we couldn't deliver is accomplished as we, instead of redoubling our own efforts, simply embrace what the Spirit is doing in us. Those who think they can do it on their own end up obsessed with measuring their own moral muscle but never get around to exercising it in real life. Those who trust God's action in them find that God's Spirit is in them—living and breathing God'!

The Bible informs about sin mainly through stories, and its most complete story of sin involves a national leader whose crimes easily over-shadow those of celebrity pop stars or footballers. The sin in question began as a spark of everyday lust by King David, perhaps the greatest leader in Israel's history, who spied a married woman bathing on a nearby rooftop. It ended in adultery and murder, as well as a needless battle that cost the lives of many soldiers.

Interestingly, the account of this notorious sin has one central theme: a broken relationship with God. *Psalm 51:4: 'Against you, you only, have I sinned,'* prayed King David after he got caught a remarkable response considering that he had just committed adultery and murder. Bathsheba, her husband and the others who died as a result of his wrongdoing faded into the background as David dealt with the most important after-effect of his misdeeds.

The theme reminded Israel that even the king reported to a higher authority, and the rest of the Bible underscores this insight into the most serious consequence of sin: it blocks contact between the natural and spiritual worlds. Sin introduces a kind of static interference in communication with God and, as a result, shuts us off from the very resource we need to combat it.

However, it does not stop God loving us. *'But God proved His love for us in that while we were still sinners Christ died for us ' (Romans 5 v 8, NRSV).*

The best analogy from my experience is that when my husband and I stayed in a cottage in Somerset, the walls were so thick that our mobile phones wouldn't work as they were unable to receive a signal. We had to step outside to make connection. Walk away from that which is blocking communication with God!

David's story, told in all its seamy detail, provides a case study of communication with the spiritual world blocked and then restored. There is no magic secret to restoring contact with God. In fact, it follows the same basic path required to restore any broken relationship, whether family, spouse or friend - the path of confession. This confession, 'I have sinned,' puts us on the same side as God. We agree with our Father that our behaviour is wrong. We are then working together with God to defeat sin in our lives.

The reason I see confession as a gift is because I received so much of my healing through belonging to a small group where we could, to use the jargon, 'struggle without shame'. When I first became a Christian, four of us came together to ask God to teach us how to pray. We began with worship and would remain worshipping until we sensed the presence of God. This was not sung worship but words of adoration and grateful thanksgiving. The presence of God led to confession, although we would not have used that word. Our confessions were very real, confessing, for example, our lying, our short tempers with our toddlers or avoidance of our mothers' phone calls! After a year to eighteen months, these three other women knew me better than I had ever known myself- not my 'image' but the real me. And they still loved me. A totally healing experience! Thirty years later we are still in the same church together.

Because of my experience of belonging to such a group, I want to encourage confessional prayer partners, groups and communities. I think accountability groups often fall short in this area, when there is no confessing, receiving the cleansing power of the blood of Jesus and consequently being powerfully and individually transformed.

Confession needs to be an ongoing discipline of regarding newly arising sins. We have all heard people's well-rehearsed conversion stories of how they were the worst of sinners. These can be of great value in the right evangelistic setting but the confession I am writing about is our failure to be all that God has called us to be in our everyday lives.

MISUNDERSTANDINGS CONCERNING CONFESSION

We can avoid confession in what appears to be a spiritual exchange. I hear conversations when someone says, 'I forgive you.' Of course, sometimes this is done within a church context where the person being forgiven doesn't even know what it is they have done! In other situations, telling someone you have forgiven them can be passive anger. It is certainly claiming the moral high ground and can be a subtle form of accusation or a sanctimonious way of telling them you hope they'll see the error of their ways.

> R T Kendall writes: 'I must add one caution: never go to a person you have had to forgive and say to them, "I forgive you ". This will be counter-productive every time unless it is to a person that you happen to know is yearning for you to forgive them. Otherwise, you will create a stir that you will not be able to cope with. They will say to you, "For what?" It is my experience that nine out of ten people I have had to forgive sincerely do not feel they have done anything wrong. It is up to me to forgive them from heart — and then keep quiet about it.'[73]

When a relationship has gone wrong we need to say sorry for our part in the breakdown. "I am sorry," is all we need to say. Even adding, "Please forgive me" can be too much as you are asking for a gift the other person may not be ready to give.

Another misunderstanding is thinking we need to confess our sins to everyone! One lady came to live in our parish and when

we went to lunch started telling me how she had had an affair
but she and her husband were now reconciled. When I asked her
why she was telling me this she replied that she wanted to live in
the light with everyone and therefore they needed to know
about her sin. I felt she didn't need to as she was forgiven and
cleansed by the blood of Jesus, forgiven by her husband and
moving forward in a new church. She had confessed her sin and
was forgiven so she didn't need to keep telling people. Having
gone through the difficult process of confession, she could let
the past be the past.

Once we have confessed to God or within our confessional
group we need to leave it behind. Often, to confess to God alone is
sufficient, but sometimes it is a habitual sin or we are suffering
from low grade guilt or shaming voices so we need someone or
others to hear our confession. '*Therefore, confess your sins to one
another that you may be healed.*' (James 5:16)

DIFFICULTIES IN CONFESSING

Sin will work in secret and loses its power only when it is
forced out into the open. Our desire to look strong and virtuous

230

keeps us from admitting to others that we have done anything wrong. We may try to blot it out from our memory, to keep it hidden, not only from others, but also from ourselves, but the effect is to pile guilt upon guilt, when all the time Jesus is 'dying' to wash us clean.

We hate confessing. We may prefer to invite someone to dinner or buy them a present than to be honest and say sorry. One pamphlet on alcoholism estimates that sobriety is 10% about alcohol and 90% about honesty. Alcoholics Anonymous have a saying, 'we remain as sick as our sickest secret'.

King David turned his humiliation into a public document, one that became enshrined in a national song (Psalm 51). To David, restoring a right relationship with God counted far more than maintaining his reputation as a ruler. Something in us resists repentance at all costs. We would rather deny, lie, blame or rationalize, anything but repent.

We want to appear respectable, to look good in front of others and to pretend that we are in control. Author Keith

Miller notes that: 'Paradoxically, honest confession before others is the only way to silence the "shaming voices" within the secrets about ourselves that we try diligently to hide.' Our secrets control us. Their power comes from the threat of revealing the shameful acts of our past. When we voluntarily share these secrets in a spiritual community says Miller, 'We break the power of the shaming voices.'[74]

Dietrich Bonhoeffer:

'In the confession of concrete sins the old man dies a painful, shameful death before the eyes of a brother. Because this humiliation is so hard we continually scheme to avoid it. Yet in the deep mental and physical pain of humiliation before another, we experience our rescue and salvation.'[75]

We visit the doctor to say what's wrong in the same way we confess, not to explain ourselves, but to cleanse ourselves.

'Christianity has at its core a most unnatural concept called GRACE, which means that we can do nothing to

counterbalance our sins. God has already paid the
penalty and we need to merely accept it by trusting him for
the remedy. Grace is God's free gift, with repentance the
way to access it.'[76]

GOOD NEWS OF CONFESSION

Ron, my husband, and I were on a mission where the
speaker invited those who wished to confess to find a prayer
team member to hear their confession. The lady who came to me
confessed for the first time ever her unfaithfulness to her
husband and the fact that one of her daughters was the result of
an adulterous affair. Unbeknown to her, at the same time, in
another part of the church, that daughter was giving her life to
Jesus. I believe something in the unseen world happened -
somehow the lady's confession to God and to me released her
daughter.

I once overheard a conversation where a little boy had
confessed that he had broken his sister's toy and hidden the
evidence. I heard the father say, 'What you did was naughty

but, now I know, you are not to worry about it anymore. Daddy will fix it.'

That is just like our heavenly Father, '*not only does He forgive us, He cleanses us from all unrighteousness.*' (1 John 1: 9)

HOW TO CONFESS

Remember, false guilt and condemnation is vague and general like a grey blanket. This non-specific feeling of condemnation is not from God! The Holy Spirit's conviction is specific, leading to release and freedom. We know what it is about so we are able to respond, 'Yes, Lord, that's true'.

The first thing to remember is: keep short accounts. I used to add things to my list to wait until I had a wheelbarrow load so I could have a long confession prayer time. This didn't work! What I learnt was not to keep thinking about whatever it was I had done but to confess it.

Whether we confess just to God, to our group or to a priest, will be partly dependent on the church we belong to, and as I have written, whether further release and healing is needed.

We need to name the sin. Words are very important; plain, simple words. We need to avoid sensational exaggeration, dramatizing small matters. We also need to avoid the opposite danger of minimizing, explaining away or rationalizing our sins. For example, we need to say, 'I lied' rather than, 'I didn't mean to be dishonest.' Bringing what we know before God without excuses and seriously asking for forgiveness, cleansing, healing and grace, results in glorious freedom.

PRAYER OF CONFESSION

Enter into the presence of God.

I often bring to mind the truth that because of the broken body of Christ, symbolized by the temple veil being torn from top to bottom, I can enter into the Holy of Holies. We need to know we can come in confidence and we need to take off all deception and attempts to hide in our old nature.

Francois Fenelon (1651-1715) wrote: 'Cut and tear and burn and destroy and spare nothing of the old flesh, of the old veil.'[77]

A W Tozer wrote:

'Take away that veil from before your face. God is taking away the one He had up to shut you out. Now you take the one you had up to shut Him out. Tear, rend, cut and burn until there is nothing left of the old veil that shuts us out from His presence.'[78]

Father God,

Thank you that Jesus is in the throne room interceding for me. Thank you that with my holy imagination I can picture that the foot of the cross is where I am standing now and the top of it reaches the Throne Room of Heaven.

I confess that I have *(name the sin or sins)* against you and against *(name who you have sinned against if relevant)* and I am sorry. Please forgive me.

WAIT (Meditate on the power of Jesus dying on the cross for you)

Father I receive your forgiveness and I ask for the blood of Jesus to cleanse me. Please set me free from the power/grip of the sin. Help me to live in the truth of your forgiveness. Amen.

Praying Psalm 51 is also helpful, knowing we can join our prayers to David's prayer in the knowledge that God answers.

Psalm 51

For the director of music. A psalm of David. When the prophet Nathan came to him after David had committed adultery with Bathsheba.

Have mercy on me, O God, according to your unfailing love; according to your great compassion blot out my transgressions.

Wash away all my iniquity and cleanse me from my sin.

For I know my transgressions, and my sin is always before me.

Against you, you only, have I sinned and done what is evil in your sight; so you are right in your verdict and justified when you judge.

Surely I was sinful at birth, sinful from the time my mother conceived me.

Yet you desired faithfulness even in the womb; you taught me wisdom in that secret place.

Cleanse me with hyssop, and I will be clean; wash me, and I will be whiter than snow.

Let me hear joy and gladness; let the bones you have crushed rejoice.

Hide your face from my sins and blot out all my iniquity.

Create in me a pure heart, O God, and renew a steadfast spirit within me.

Do not cast me from your presence or take your Holy Spirit from me.

Restore to me the joy of your salvation and grant me a willing spirit, to sustain me.

Then I will teach transgressors your ways, so that sinners will turn back to you.

Deliver me from the guilt of bloodshed, O God, you who are God my Savior, and my tongue will sing of your righteousness.

Open my lips, Lord, and my mouth will declare your praise.

You do not delight in sacrifice, or I would bring it; you do not take pleasure in burnt offerings.

My sacrifice, O God, is a broken spirit; a broken and contrite heart you, God, will not despise.

May it please you to prosper Zion, to build up the walls of Jerusalem. Then you will delight in the sacrifices of the righteous, in burnt offerings offered whole; then bulls will be offered on your altar.

RECEIVING FORGIVENESS

As counsellors or church leaders we often hear, 'I know God forgives me but I can't forgive myself.' God loves us as much as those we have forgiven, and He doesn't want us to continue to hold anything against ourselves anymore than He wants us to continue to hold judgement against others.

When someone is struggling with the 'I can't forgive myself', I prefer to emphasize receiving God's forgiveness.

Paraphrasing an extract from Rosemary Green's ' *God's Catalyst':* Many counsellors emphasize the need to forgive ourselves. It is important that we are not weighed down with guilt and regret. But the "I must forgive myself has a basic flaw when it stems from a theory that has no room for God, no understanding of the cross. Without the cross there is no place to leave the guilt; with the cross it is blasphemy to hang onto the guilt.

Receiving forgiveness is a decision of the will. We choose to agree with God's verdict and see ourselves as forgiven. If the

241

King of Kings, the Creator of the Universe declares us not guilty, who are we not to forgive! We are, in effect, saying God may have forgiven me but my pride won't let me do the same. We may not feel forgiven but then we have to educate our feelings. As I have written elsewhere, feelings are like children, they need to be listened to, nurtured and educated, but we are not to be defined by them.

If someone is struggling to receive their forgiveness I may ask "If you could relive that moment would you do it again?" The answer is always "Oh no!" We may not be given the opportunity to change or to know we have changed but Joseph's brothers were when in the story I referred to in Chapter 4, Joseph put the cup in Benjamin's sack. This was loving and kind in that it gave the opportunity for change. Joseph did it to test the depth and sincerity of his brothers' repentance. They had admitted their guilt in Genesis 42:21 but there are two kinds of repentance: when we are sorry because we have been caught out, or when we have a real change of mind and heart. So Joseph gave them the opportunity to do away with Benjamin, just as they had done away with him. After all, in Genesis 42:38

Jacob virtually says that if Benjamin is killed he will have no-one. The brothers had every reason to continue to be jealous as Jacob obviously favoured Benjamin, son of Rachel, over all his other sons by Leah and the concubines.

Have you a problem with guilt? You've confessed and confessed, know that God has forgiven you but still feel guilty? We have all done things we wished we had not, made wrong decisions, done things that we hoped no-one would find out about. The kindest thing that could ever happen is to find that we would not do it again. That was the gift Joseph gave his brothers. Joseph tested his brothers but now they were so changed. This time Judah offered his life for Benjamin.[79]

We need to focus on what Jesus has done for us rather than what we have done to Him. There is often an inability to receive forgiveness whereby we are caught in a cycle of continually confessing, repenting and hating ourselves, unable to look up to Jesus on the cross and receive.

I was faced with this issue in a very stark way. I was attending a service where one of my friends was being baptized by immersion. She was a recovering alcoholic. I knew I would be part of the baptized person's testimony. The night before I inadvertently had too much to drink and was suffering from a hangover. I repented then started condemning myself, then hating myself, followed by more regret, remorse and repenting. Then God spoke to me and said I had a choice - I could focus on what I had done the previous evening or on what Jesus had done for me at the cross, the choice was mine.

When we suffer from introspection there are two positions that stop us receiving forgiveness, either the grandiose promoting of the false self or the self-abasing, shamed, false humility self. Whichever position we hide in, God gives us the same choice. 'Choose for yourselves this day whom you will serve'. (Joshua 24: 15). Conviction is specific, offering a way out, "Yes, Lord, that is true". It is a relief.

The inability to let go of past sins for which we have already repented can lead to frustration and despair. Soren Kierkegaard wrote this prayer:

'Dear Father, hold not our sins up against us, but hold us up against our sins, so that the thought of You -when it wakens in our soul ... should not remind us of what we have committed, but of what You did forgive, not of how we went astray, but of how You did save us.'[80]

So when past sin comes to haunt us, we need to redirect our thinking from our sin to that of God's saving grace, that enabled us to walk away free.

Love keeps no record of wrongs and nor should we. This story illustrates this truth:

'A little boy was visiting his grandparents and given a catapult to play with. He practiced in the woods, but he could never hit his target. As he came back to Grandma's backyard, he saw her pet duck. Just out of impulse he took aim and let fly. The stone hit and the duck fell dead. The boy panicked. Desperately he hid the dead duck in the wood pile, only to look up and see his sister watching. Sally had seen it all, but she said nothing. After lunch that day, Grandma said, "Sally, let's wash the dishes ". But Sally said, "Johnny told me he wanted to help in the kitchen today, didn't you Johnny?" And she whispered to him, "Remember the duck!" So Johnny did the dishes. Later Grandpa asked if the children wanted to go fishing. Grandma said, "I'm sorry, but I need Sally to help make supper". Sally smiled and said, "That's all taken care of, Johnny wants to do it. "Again she whispered, "Remember the duck". Johnny stayed while Sally went fishing.

After several days of Johnny doing both his chores and Sally's, finally he couldn't stand it. He confessed to Grandma that he'd killed the duck. "I know, Johnny" she said, giving him a hug. "I was standing at the window and saw the whole thing. Because I love you, I forgave you. I was just wondering how long you would let Sally make a slave of you.[81]

RECEIVING COMPLETE FORGIVENESS

Wherever we fantasize 'how we could have done it better' we are clinging to the wrong and we write a record of wrongs about ourselves.

We can wake up reliving past failures, mistakes and sins, with all of the subsequent guilt, but we need to remember that either our unhealed self or the enemy is taking advantage of us and tempting us to believe a lie. We need to experience the love that keeps no record of wrongs. We need to not be defined by our past. What if Moses had said, 'You can't use me, I am a murderer'? Or Peter, 'You can't use me, I will let you down'? Receive forgiveness and close the door on the past.

6

Forgiveness is one of the hardest steps we need to take as

an obedient follower of Jesus, but also one of the most freeing

and releasing. Forgiveness is about giving a pardon, it is a gift.

Forgiveness means to remit, let off, to cease to hold

resentment, anger or bitterness towards a person or about an

offence. It also means to grant release from payment of a debt.

Forgiveness means 'to hurl away, to free yourself.' We need to

forgive everything from the small misdemeanour or discourtesy

through to the most grievous of sins.

Forgiveness is extremely difficult. It feels unnatural, wrong

and goes against the grain. Nor does it automatically put an end

to the matter; long after we have forgiven we may still have the

memory and pain of the injury. This does not necessarily mean

that our forgiveness has been inadequate. I believe that if we

find forgiveness easy we have either loved superficially or

forgiven superficially. As it is a gift we extend to others, we first need to be a receiver of the gift. It is only as we understand how much we have been forgiven that we are able to forgive. As we live in the stream of Christ's forgiveness to us, as we receive His grace and mercy, we have something to give others.

As the Lord's prayer says:

'*Forgive us our sins, as we forgive those who sin against us.*' It is a receiving and giving.

SPIRITUAL BENEFITS

In the following verses we can see a strong correlation between receiving our Father's forgiveness for our sins and forgiving others.

Matthew 18:35

'*If you forgive those who sin against you, your heavenly Father will forgive you. But if you refuse to forgive others your Father will not forgive your sins.*'

Colossians 3:13

'You must make allowance for each other's faults and forgive the person who offends you. Remember the Lord forgave you say you must forgive others.'

The abbot Macarius said, 'If we dwell upon the harms that have been wrought on us by men, we amputate from our mind the power of dwelling on God.' [82]

One of my main motivations for forgiving others, as hard as it may be, is my desire to remain forgiven by God. We can forgive only when we know what Jesus death on the cross has done for us and the clear connection that God forgives my debts as I forgive my debtor. Fortunately we do not struggle alone. The Holy Spirit comes and leads us into all truth, comforts us, makes us strong where we are weak - Jesus says in John 14:16 -17a.

'And I will ask the Father, and he will give you another Counsellor (Comforter) who will never leave you. He is the Holy Spirit, who leads into all truth.'

Therefore, with the empowering presence of the Holy Spirit within us, we can choose to forgive.

George Macdonald writes, 'It may be infinitely worse to refuse to forgive than to murder, because the latter may be an impulse of a moment of heat, whereas the former is a cold and deliberate choice of the heart.' [83]

While William Blake writes, more positively, 'Mutual forgiveness of each vice such of the Gates of Paradise.'[84]

Another spiritual benefit is that forgiveness is a good weapon in our spiritual warfare. Forgiveness protects us from the work of the enemy. St Paul writes of this in his second letter to the Corinthians, chapter 2 (The Message):

'Now, regarding the one who started all this - the person in question who caused all this pain - I want you to know that I am not the one injured in this as much as, with a few exceptions, all of you. So I don't want to come down too hard. What the majority of you agreed to as punishment is punishment enough. Now is the time to

forgive this man and help him back on his feet. If all you do is pour on the guilt, you could very well drown him in it. My counsel now is to pour on the love.

The focus of my letter wasn't on punishing the offender but on getting you to take responsibility for the health of the church. So if you forgive him, I forgive him. Don't think I'm carrying around a list of personal grudges. The fact is that I'm joining in with YOUR forgiveness, as Christ is with us, guiding us. After all, we don't want to unwittingly give Satan an opening for yet more mischief - we're not oblivious to his sly ways!'

When we don't forgive, Satan gets in. When there is a breakdown of relationships in the Body of Christ it is like an unprotected wound. A graphic picture would be an injured soldier lying in the desert being attacked by flies. Forgiveness covers the wound so the enemy has no landing place! Where there is personal unforgiveness, Satan will exploit self-pity and feed our bitterness. He takes advantage of our unforgiveness and can ride on top of it, causing us to believe the lie that we are justified in our unforgiveness. Satan is the father of lies.

HEALTH BENEFITS

As well as spiritual reasons for forgiving others there are also health issues.

Edward Hallowell, psychologist, was involved in a five-year study of 1,000 patients looking at the health benefits of psychological well-being. He concluded that unforgiveness may cause high blood pressure, weakened immune system, headaches, backaches, neck pain, as well as a weakened sexual self. He felt this was linked to indicators that forgiveness boosts the immune system by reducing production of the 'stress hormone' Cortisol. He concluded that the hostility combined with the suppressing and repressing of anger and the desire for revenge was physically toxic. He wrote of the need to encourage people to let go of past wrongs - what the Bible calls 'forgiveness.'[85]

In 5 June 2000 issue of London's *Daily Express* there appeared an article with this headline: 'Can you learn to forgive?' The opening words were these: 'Bearing a grudge can hold you back and even damage your health.' The writer of the article, Susan Pape, had interviewed Dr Ken Hart, Lecturer at Leeds University, who had been running the 'world's first forgiveness course,' designed to help people forgive their enemies and let go of grudges. Participants ranged from victims of burglary, to jilted husbands, to those who have been bullied. All had one thing in common: they were angry, bitter and wanted revenge.

Forgiveness has been recognised as valid and therapeutic even outside the realm of the Christian faith. The reason for this course in Leeds, which was paid for by a £120,000 grant from the John Templeton Foundation, was apparently because forgiving can be good for your health. Holding a grudge, it is said, leads to illnesses ranging from common colds to heart disease because of all the stored up anger and stress. Dr Sandi Mann, a psychologist at the University of Central Lancashire, believes that there is a strong link between our emotions and our immune system. All this goes to demonstrate the benefits of forgiving people - even if someone is not motivated by Jesus and the New Testament! Indeed, here are ten steps to Freedom, as found in the Daily Express's article: [86]

1. *Stop excusing, pardoning or rationalising.*

2. *Pinpoint the actions that have hurt you.*

3. *Spend time thinking of ways in which one's life would be more satisfying if you could let go of your grievances.*

4. *Try replacing angry thoughts about the 'badness' of the perpetrator with thoughts about how the offender is also a human being who is vulnerable to harm.*

5. *Identifying yourself with the offender's probable state of mind. Understand the perpetrator's history while not condoning his or her actions.*

6. *Spend some time developing greater compassion towards the perpetrator.*

7. *Become more aware that you have needed other people's forgiveness in the past.*

8. *Make a heartfelt resolution not to pass on one's own pain.*

9. *Spend time appreciating the sense of purpose and direction that comes after steps 1 to 8.*

10. *Enjoy the sense of emotional relief that comes when the burden of a grudge has melted away. Enjoy also the feeling of goodwill and mercy you have shown.*

FUTURE BENEFITS

Forgiveness means, 'You took my yesterdays, you cannot have my tomorrows.'

We need to understand that forgiveness unlocks our future from our past. As I have acknowledged, forgiveness does not always bring completion because the pain and hurt may not immediately disappear, but as we forgive, the results of the injury lose their grip on us and are taken over by God, who knows what to do!

Forgiveness breaks the vicious circle of blame and pain. If the circle remains unbroken, resentment results, which literally means 'to feel again'. Resentment leads to going over and over in our mind what they did. It is like allowing uninvited guests to live in our house rent free, recounting, and reliving exactly what happened. Instead of giving us release and relief it does the exact opposite. Resentment clings to the past, picking each fresh scab so the wound never heals. Forgiveness offers a way out. It does not settle questions of blame or fairness but unless we break the cycle we would remain stuck in the past and bound to the people we cannot forgive. We are held in their vice grip. Not to forgive imprisons us in the past and locks up all potential for change. We thus yield control to another and condemn ourselves to suffer the consequences of the sin.

The following two stories illustrate this well.

A friend of mine, Clay Mclean, [87] tells the story of a confrontation he had with a lady after he had spoken on unforgiveness. He had driven a long way to teach and minister at a large meeting. At midnight, exhausted, just as he was about to get into his car for the long drive home, a very irate, upset lady approached him shouting, 'How dare you. How dare you speak on forgiveness. I was sexually abused by my father from a young age and raped by my two brothers as a teenager and you dare to speak of forgiveness.' Clay, tired, and not knowing what to do or say, asked the Holy Spirit to help him. He replied, 'Yes, and unless you forgive them they will be in bed with you again tonight.'

Philip Yancey tells another equally powerful story of a Rabbi. Having survived the Holocaust, the Rabbi decided to emigrate to the USA. At Immigration control he told the officer, 'I had to forgive Hitler - I did not want him to come to my new country with me.'[88]

Resentment poisons us, unforgiveness imprisons us. 'To forgive is to set a prisoner free and discover the prisoner is you.'[89]

BARRIERS TO FORGIVING OTHERS

1. Not understanding our own need to confess to God and receive forgiveness. We extend forgiveness as forgiven sinners.

2. Not trusting God's justice. Forgiveness is an act of faith. By forgiving another we are trusting God is a better justice maker than we are. By forgiving, we release our own right to get even and leave all issues of fairness to God to work out. We can see forgiveness as our referring the case to a higher court. This does involve a risk, however; the risk that God may not deal with the person as we would want. The prophet Jonah, for instance, resented God for being more merciful than he thought the Ninevites deserved. We are like this. When it is us 'in the dock' we want and ask for forgiveness, grace and mercy. We think

about God being slow to anger and abounding in love. When we send someone else to God's court we focus on God's justice, what we think is fair and how we think they should be treated as they deserve, receive 'their just deserts'.

3. Clinging to our rights: 'How things should be.' (See chapter 4)

4. Fear: When we have separation anxiety, which can be described as feelings of lostness, disconnection, non-being and fear of abandonment, [90] we cling to anything, even if it is toxic. The fear of 'letting go' and forgiving is extreme. A lie is believed - that nursing sins against us and clinging to the right to get even is preferable to having nothing to hold on to.

Fear causes confusion. Forgiveness does not always mean forgetting. It means remembering without rancour (a rancid heart). Nor does it preclude further action.

There is also a fear that forgiveness has to include reconciliation. Obviously in some circumstances reconciliation may be desirable but not in all and it is not always possible. The fear comes from the thought, 'What if I forgive them and they do it again?' Forgiving someone does not mean we cannot set healthy boundaries.[91] If the person hasn't changed and will continue to sin against us, it is sensible to distance ourselves. There is a difference between forgiving and condoning the sin, or colluding with the sin.

A young man, as a recovering alcoholic, realised that one of the triggers for his drinking was visiting his verbally abusive father. Feeling bad about himself and angry with his father, his desire to avoid these painful feelings led him to drink. Martin continually forgave his father and understood that until he was stronger in dealing with his own emotions; clear boundaries would have to be put in place.

His plan of action was two-fold. When possible, he would visit with a friend or meet his father in a neutral, public place - no unaccompanied home visits. If in any of these more secure situations his father began abusing him, Martin would say, 'I don't have to listen to this,' and leave. This required a lot of practice as confronting a powerful parent is very scary. This plan did not negate the truth that Martin had forgiven his father and continued to walk in forgiveness towards his father after every fresh incident.

The confusion between boundaries and forgiveness is often seen in church life. This was highlighted when a vicar asked me to see the wife of his youth leader. Simon had been on staff and was very popular within the youth outreach. He had been a drug addict but was now clean. However, the pressure of his job, marriage and three children proved too much. With the exposure to drugs because of his youth outreach work, he fell into temptation. This culminated in his running away. When Carole, his wife, came to see me it transpired that for six years she had been a victim of abuse and physical violence. The extent of this was such that I encouraged her to go on the 'at risk' list at the police station. We then heard he had been sent to prison for attacking someone. Carole had by this time been able to completely forgive him. When the church heard he was in prison, Carole was put under some pressure to visit him. She refused, saying it wasn't safe, she was told she needed to forgive him. There was confusion between forgiveness and the need for boundaries, by church members. Reconciliation was not possible at that time.

5. Wanting the person to acknowledge they have sinned: If we are honest, most of us only want to forgive people who are sorry! One of my children, when he was young, said he did not want to forgive his friend until the friend knew how much he had upset him and was sorry. We are like this, although we may use more 'grown-up' language, such as; 'I have yet to see the fruits of repentance.' Although we need to see change for full reconciliation to occur, we cannot put that condition on forgiveness. Jesus forgives before we know we need it. Even when dying he said to those crucifying him, '*Forgive them, Father, they know not what they do.*' Luke 23:34

Likewise, as hard as it is, we need to forgive even when the person shows no remorse or denies what has happened. We also struggle when they continually insist they have done nothing wrong. Remember that our unforgiveness keeps us imprisoned.

6. Forgiveness and Identity: Sometimes when we seek revenge, unforgiveness can so fuel our thinking and view of ourselves that to forgive feels as though it threatens our identity. One young man, Peter, faced such a dilemma. He had been fostered by unloving 'parents' who wanted a playmate for their only son.

The foster mother had been particularly cold and unloving towards him. She never believed him and always favoured her natural born son when there were any squabbles. When Peter came to see me he was ambivalent towards women, felt outside of society and wanted (he claimed) to stay on the outside. After some sessions I suggested we look at the issue of forgiving his foster mother. His reply was, 'What will I live on?' 'What will feed me?' 'What would I think about?' He was saying, in effect, 'How will I exist without nursing resentment and revenge?' His identity, sense of existence and self were completely shaped by his imposed prisoner food. He had become institutionalised by his own unforgiveness. He was enmeshed in his responses to past wrongs.

Another lady, Sarah, had a similar response. Her parents had wanted a boy and had never really been able to nurture her. They had favoured their nephew and in reaction to this she had made her own identity. She had responded by emotionally rejecting them and successfully becoming her own person. She was a 'self-made' woman. When I suggested she needed to forgive her parents she said, 'But who will I be? To forgive them would erode my identity. I feel I would no longer exist.' This is also true with confession where we have defined ourselves by our own sin, for example, 'I am an adulterer' not, 'I was unfaithful.'

INABILITY TO NAME THE SIN

Deprivation

It is difficult to forgive something or someone when we cannot actually name what was done to us. This is particularly true where there has been emotional deprivation. One lady, Lucy, began forgiving her father, although she didn't know what for. She just knew the relationship wasn't right and having confessed her wrong attitude towards him, she began to forgive him - but for what? Eventually she came to understand that although he was physically present he was emotionally absent. She then forgave him for not being a father to her, the sin of omission. This process took about a year and I will write more about that process later.

Deprivation is not easily acknowledged as there is some truth in the saying, 'What you never have you never miss.' After the second world war, bananas are something that young children had never seen or eaten. Whilst not missing them, it would be true to say that their diet was not as varied as those who had not been rationed.

It is also difficult to recognise deprivation or neglect when we are told we had a happy childhood or a privileged background. These statements usually mean we were materially looked after, and 'privileged' often means we had a good education. Having been told this, our sense that all is not well just makes us feel guilty and that there is something wrong with us. There is an added difficulty if our siblings seem satisfied and happy.

When others like the offender

Alan was an extremely popular, charismatic figure, a professor
at a prestigious university. He was a lively member of his church
and was always available to take any visiting Christians around
the college on a very entertaining tour. Behind closed doors,
however, he was cold and indifferent. His wife's desire for
intimacy was interpreted by Alan as being needy. For her to
believe in herself and begin the journey of truth and forgiveness
was enormous. Her constant nagging doubt was 'everyone else
likes him so I must be wrong.'

She also had to forgive those on the church leadership team she
tentatively tried to speak to, who saw her as exaggerating or
'making a fuss about nothing.'

Recognising Control

When we find ourselves continually forgiving the same
person or persons in the same circumstances there is usually an
underlying problem. When we lack self - responsibility and fear

take control of our lives - we give responsibility to others and allow them to control us.

If we see ourselves as of little value we may hold irrational beliefs such as, 'friends only like me when I fit in.' 'Parents accept me when I fulfil their expectations.' 'My partner loves me because I "dance" around him and try to meet all his needs.' God expects us to have self-control and take responsibility for ourselves.' We may however, despite all our efforts to take responsibility for our own lives, be in relationship with a very controlling person. The sin against us is particularly difficult to own if it is benevolent control. If someone is genuinely doing what they think is best for us, but not allowing us to make decisions for ourselves, we experience an enormous mixture of emotions. We feel grateful they are concerned for our welfare, are looking after us, but we feel angry that they are taking over. We then feel guilty for our anger because they only have our best interests at heart.

Whether it is malevolent or benevolent control, the issue is exposed when we try to talk about it. The more manipulated we feel, especially when there is a 'moving of the goalposts' or an altered version of the events, the more we need to face the fact that we are being sinned against by being controlled. If the controller is also very articulate, we can end up feeling shamed, confused and tongue-tied.

AVOIDANCE OF NAMING SIN

We often try to evade naming sin because the reality can be painful. Avoidance has a variety of expressions:

a) Generalisation

Often people will come to see me making statements like, 'This church is unfriendly.' I then have to ask questions like 'Who'? 'What'? 'Where'? 'When'? in order to help the person actually name the offence.

b) Distortion

We distort the facts often preferring to blame ourselves. Taking false responsibility may feel easier than confronting the other person, if we have a fear of conflict. This is also true where we feel indebted to the person, which may overlap with the control issues.

c) Rationalisation

This is often the, 'Well, everyone did/does it, so it can't have been wrong to do that to me.' One lady during a prayer for the healing of the memories had a picture of herself at about six years old, sitting outside a pub on her own. I suggested perhaps this wasn't the best of parenting. She replied, "No, everyone did that in those days." She was my age and was very upset with me when I explained that I had never been left outside a pub. Avoiding the pain of her childhood by rationalising felt better than facing the reality.

A more disturbing incident was when I was on a mission in a culture that included a lot of sexual abuse; one lady could not see that her uncle had sinned against her because it was 'only molestation.'

d) Denial

Those of us who do not deny the bad memories, betrayals and pain inflicted upon us; may instead deny that it has affected us. It is statements such as, 'I know it happened to me but there is nothing wrong with me.'

e) Condoning

This is the most common form of avoidance when we need to acknowledge having been sinned against. It shows itself in statements such as, 'He was tired, he didn't really mean it.' This may be true but understanding the reason doesn't constitute forgiveness. 'She had a damaged childhood so I am sure she didn't mean it or doesn't know any better.' This is loving and understanding but isn't forgiveness. It easily slips into condoning someone else's sin against us, or 'turning a blind eye.' It is true that every person is worth understanding but that does not excuse them.

f) Inability to name sin as sin

Our politically correct language, whilst doing some good in helping to eradicate offensive language in terms of gender and racism, has also silenced many aspects of the word 'sin.' 'Cancer' was a word that, in the past, was avoided because it was a death sentence. Nowadays, because there has been much medical advancement and cure, the word is less scary. People who are not Christians do not like the word 'sin' for much the same reason. They do not know that to name, confess and forgive sin is healing and releasing. I once saw a church noticeboard proclaiming 'Come back sin - all is forgiven.' Brilliant! Jesus did not die for our 'unhealthy' attitudes, actions and relationships; He died for our sinful ones!

FEELINGS

Forgiveness is an act of the will. If I wait until I feel like forgiving someone I will probably wait forever! However, even though it is a will decision we cannot discount our feelings. There is a saying, 'Without forgiveness feelings get buried alive.'[92] They start smelling, becoming rancid, rotting and seeping out in other ways. These feelings, unlike champagne, do not improve with age! We have to let the cork out before it goes sour. We need to release the inflamed feelings and infected attitudes caused by past hurts. Feelings need to be identified, described, confessed and shared. We can do this through a variety of different creative ways such as visualising, role-play, journalling or writing a letter to the offender. If the latter, don't send it! Feelings often have an energy in them that needs to be released. This can include crying, shouting, going for a walk or spring cleaning the house!

When this is done in a non-judgemental atmosphere, or with a wise, safe person, it is like a healing, soothing medicine.

As I have written, feelings that are suppressed (buried) or denied usually turn to hate, envy, jealousy or bitterness. We need to ask God to bring true insight to help identify hurt feelings and locked up emotions. The Holy Spirit can reveal and heal these feelings and bring release from this 'prison.'

IDENTIFY UNFORGIVENESS

All of the following insights have come from my experience. You may be able to add some more.

a) If we keep rehearsing, checking, going over in our minds the bad things that the person has done in the past and waiting for more evidence to add to the list, we know there is a forgiveness issue.

b) Using our imaginations to distort or add to known events or sins is evidence of the need to forgive. We can also rehearse other scenarios whereby the person continues to sin against us and add that to the list.

c) When we can't get what they did off our minds and we fantasise what we might say to them or who we might tell. This is particularly damaging to us when we rehearse confrontations with controlling, articulate people, and in our imaginations become powerless again.

d) Resenting the person's success and being pleased and rejoicing if things go wrong for them, also, adding anger to our unforgiveness when things go right for them.

e) When we are unforgiving we can also instigate subtle criticism and gossip. We focus on the person's faults. We can become very deceitful in this by agreeing wholeheartedly when a compliment is paid about a person but then smuggling in a little negative. For instance, someone may say, 'He is a great preacher isn't he?' We reply, 'Amazing, absolutely brilliant. It is such a pity he is not a very good pastor and is socially awkward. Still, I expect he is shy.'

f) I always know when there has been some falling out in our church when, before a big event someone will casually ask me if someone particular will be there. There can be withdrawing from the person. This may be physically or it can be emotional avoidance. I once suggested to someone that they really needed to forgive their father. To which they replied, 'Forgive him? Why should I do that? I never think about him. It is as though he doesn't exist.' I always know when there has been a falling out in our church between two people when before a big event, someone will casually ask me if someone in particular will be there because they want to avoid them.

g) When we stop being generous toward someone this is often a sign of our lack of forgiveness. This lack of generosity isn't necessarily concerning gifts, but can be time or information. It is a general attitude of no longer wanting that person to share in our good fortune.

TIMING

Although a general principle is that forgiveness should be immediate, and this is certainly true of minor hurts and irritations, there are other considerations. Where there is a gaping wound of grievous sin against someone instant forgiveness acts more like an ineffective sticking plaster and can be used as a form of spiritual denial. One young lady, Ginnie, came to see me, who during her gap year in South America had been raped. She belonged to a lovely Christian family who had asked some trusted Christian friends to pray with her. They led her into a time of forgiveness, which I do not doubt was genuine. She went to university immediately following this and was home within six months suffering from anorexia. Whenever I tried to talk about the rape she would reply, "But I have forgiven him." She had not, however, got in touch with any of her feelings and was now using the forgiveness prayer as a means of suppressing her feelings and staying in denial.

When helping those with serious sins against them, I find it helpful to say something like, 'you do know eventually you will need to begin to forgive them.'

Even when we have begun immediately, not waiting until we feel like it, there still needs to be a continually. It is a process - but it is not like the therapy process of theory or the idea that the process itself is a permanent state. It is a relationship with Jesus and God the Father who is with us, helping us and understanding.

I normally pray, I am forgiving with my will, please make it a reality in my heart. It is the heart surgery that takes the time.

The first time I began to forgive someone, which I did every day, I found that the relationship with the person got worse. For one thing I kept remembering new painful memories, but also the ones I had forgiven seemed to feel more alive. I decided I must be doing something wrong until I read C. S. Lewis saying the seventy times seven may be for the same person and the same offence.[93]

I was teaching in Egypt on the need to continually forgive someone when after the meeting a young man came to explain to me that in Egypt it was impossible. He said they had a saying, 'Once yes, twice maybe, three times never.' I later discovered this view had very ancient roots and some of the rabbis during Jesus time would have taught this. In Matthew 18:21-22 Peter asks, '*Lord, how often should I forgive someone who sins against me? Seven times'?" No, not seven times," Jesus replied, "but seventy times seven!"* From Peter's background, seven would have been an enormous amount. Then of course, Jesus replied, seventy times seven!!

Steps to Forgiveness

1. Be honest. Confess your reluctance to forgive, your negative feelings. Tell God and ask for His help.

2. Make a choice to release the bitterness and poison.

3. Ask for God's view of the person you are forgiving.

4. Confess the sin where you have harboured bitterness and anger. Ask for forgiveness where you have blamed God. Ask Him to cleanse and heal your poisoned heart.

5. Forgive the person and ask God to bless them. (Prayers on the following pages)

6. Ask God to give you a love for the person.

7. Ask God to heal the wounds in both of you and to melt away any remaining hardness in your heart.

8. Ask God if there is any specific step you need to take.

9. If it is helpful apologize for your part - simply 'I am sorry.' As I wrote in Chapter 5, unless a person is yearning to know that

you have forgiven them it is counter-productive to say, 'I forgave you.' In my experience most people I have had to forgive do not know or feel that they have done anything wrong. I need to not bear a grudge, not take offence and forgive them from my heart and either keep quiet about it or if I believe I am partly responsible, apologize.

10. Know that as well as immediately and continually, there is a finally. One day we wake up and know, even if there is no likelihood of complete reconciliation, that it is done. It is finished. Our hearts are full of love and compassion for the person and we strongly want the best for them and for God to bless them.

Forgiveness Prayer

Dear Father, I come before you asking you will remind me of all Jesus has done for me on the cross. Help me to live in the stream of forgiveness Jesus extends to me and to receive this forgiveness as a gift. Reveal to me the depth of love you have for me as a forgiven sinner and help me to give away that which I have received. I confess to you my not wanting to forgive, my feelings and my fear but with my will I am going to choose to forgive. Amen

Prayer to Trust

Dear Father, I know I would find it easier to forgive if I felt you would deal with them according to my idea of justice. Father, I confess I like your grace and mercy for me but I do not want it for my enemies. I know this is wrong so please forgive me and help me to trust in you. Help me to refer (forgive) my offenders to your court knowing it is a court of grace and mercy. And Father, I ask you to so work in my heart that eventually I will be able to trust your verdict. Amen

Prayer for Fear

Father God, I bring to you my fear that if I forgive I will be hurt again, used and abused again. Father, I bring to you my fear that you are not taking what has happened to me seriously if 'I just forgive.' Please grant me wisdom to understand the difference between forgiveness and boundaries. Help me to not be cowardly in avoidance or foolish in unwise action. Give me insight into how far reconciliation is possible. Please also protect me from the well-meaning pressure of friends who want to see everything quickly restored.

Amen

Identity

Father, I bring to you the fear that if I forgive I will no longer know what I think or who I am. I confess I have endlessly rehearsed conversations and imaginations of revenge. I confess I have closed and detached my heart from the offenders, and living any other way is very frightening. Please help me.

Amen

Naming sin

Father God, please help me to stop avoiding, minimizing or pretending

everything is all right. I recognize I do not like living in reality. I understand

that everyone needs to be understood but making excuses for others is not

forgiveness. Please unwrap me from the layers of condoning, explaining,

rationalizing and denying so that I can be healed by you as I forgive those

who have sinned against me. Please help me to accept they have sinned so I

can forgive them. Amen

Feelings

Father, I bring my bitter, angry, resentful feelings and attitudes to you. I

confess my jealousy where those who have sinned against me continue to

prosper. I know it is me that I am damaging by continuing in unforgiveness,

not them. I understand the first prayer of forgiveness may not bring

emotional healing but I choose now not to be defined by my feelings any

more but to be obedient to your will for my life. Amen

Prayer of Forgiveness

Father God, I now come to you and ask that by the power of the Holy Spirit you will manifest Jesus to me.

(It may help at this point to hold the person in a clenched fist and as you pray slowly open your hand to give the person to Jesus) Now pray: -

Lord Jesus, I forgive (name the offender) for (name the sin) against me. I give them to you. Please come and unbind me from the effects of their sin against me. Take all the critical words they have spoken over me, all violence and abuse towards me and all the injustice I have experienced (add your own words here). I choose to see all of their sin going towards you Jesus on the cross.

Thank you your cross is like a magnet which attracts sin as I forgive. I pray now you will heal me where the sin against me has wounded and shaped me. Please loose me from all the consequences of their sin. Amen

POST FORGIVENESS

One of the difficulties of forgiveness is the different levels of the offences and therefore the different facets of action. Whilst all sin and all wrong actions are an offence against God, not all offences are committed against God alone. Some break the law and others are committed against us personally.

When the offence is against God alone then repentance is to God alone. Confession and forgiveness should be as public or private as the offence. When the offence is against the law we need to understand the importance of embracing '*loving mercy*' and acting justly (Micah 6:8).

There are many stories, particularly in the church, where children have been abused and the perpetrators of the sin have been forgiven without public accusation only to find others have subsequently been abused.

Philosopher Edmund Burke says, 'The only thing necessary for the triumph of evil is for good men to do nothing.'[94]

284

When the offence is against the law i.e. rape, burglary, attack, violence then our personal forgiveness does not negate the law of the land. By choosing to forgive we do not condone what has happened. There is no dichotomy between forgiveness and praying for legal justice.

When the sin is against us personally we need to accept the truth of the evidence and forgive the offender (see prayers).

Further Post forgiveness treatment

As I have already written, forgiveness does not automatically bring the healing we need. If someone were to shoot me in the foot and I forgave the attacker, I would still have the bullet in my foot.

We may also need help with setting boundaries when we realize we are being controlled.

There is also what I believe to be erroneous teaching concerning forgiving God. We looked at suffering in chapter 4 but I think it is worth restating that Romans 8: 28 says, '*And we know that God causes everything to work together for the good of those who love God and are called according to his purpose for them.*'

God does turn evil into good. God did not send Jesus into the world to explain evil but to save us and exemplify suffering. One day all will become clear - one day we will be able to say God has done all things well. In the meantime, we need to trust Him and take Him at his word. I think to forgive Him, even though as the argument goes, His shoulders are big enough, diminishes our faith. Rather we need to confess/express our anger and bitterness towards Him and then listen for His response.

Where we have nursed revenge and 'reinvented ourselves' the subsequent feelings of lostness, emptiness and non-being, need the Sense of Being prayers.[95]

Because confession and forgiveness are so intertwined further treatment may be involved.

Confession of own resentment, bitterness and sinful judging and sinful reaction. 'See to it that no one misses the grace of God and that no bitter root grows up to cause trouble and defile many.' (Hebrews 12:15)

We judge in the areas where we have been hurt - neglected. Even after we have forgiven, which we need to keep doing, we need to repent of our own sin of nursing resentment. We need to give God permission to dig the garden of our heart. We are not to root around, introspect, worry or strive but we need to give God permission to expose those places where we have judged and hold bitterness or continue in a sinful reaction.

Difficulties in receiving forgiveness

In the same way as we struggle to receive God's forgiveness, we often struggle to believe someone else has really forgiven us. We can be like Joseph's brothers, unsure we have been forgiven. Joseph chose to forgive and in a remarkable statement he said to his brothers '*Now therefore, be not grieved nor angry with yourselves.*' (Genesis 45:5). So not only did Joseph forgive his brothers, he encourages them to stop blaming themselves. The bible says that Joseph weeps when he recognizes them but in order to see Benjamin, accuses them of being spies and puts them in prison. He can hear how they see everything as a punishment for what they had done when they sold Joseph into slavery (see Chapter 4). Realizing now that they blame themselves, he weeps again. He then blesses them with grain provision for the journey and returns their money.

Next time when they return with Benjamin and the money, which they attempt to give back, Joseph invites them to his palace for a feast, (Genesis 43:29). Overcome with love for his brother, Joseph rushes out to hide his emotions.

We then have the incident with the cup in Benjamin's sack, which I wrote about in the previous chapter. The incident that caused them to know how much they had changed. Now when they come back again, Joseph can stand it no longer - he sends his servants out and reveals himself saying, "*But don't be upset, and don't be angry with yourselves for selling me to this place. It was God who sent me here ahead of you to preserve your lives.*" (Genesis 45:5)

His forgiveness was so complete that he did not want to shame them, nor did he want them to continually blame themselves and live under condemnation so he sent his servants out. However, Joseph's brothers despite all of Joseph's forgiveness are still insecure in receiving their forgiveness.

This becomes evident when their father dies, frightened they say, *'Joseph will pay us back for all the evil we did to him.'* (Genesis 50:15) They send him a message claiming their father had instructed Joseph to forgive them. Joseph cries out - then speaks kindly to them reassuring them with the amazing statement, *'As far as I am concerned God turned into good what you meant for evil.'* (Genesis 50:20)

Joseph had not only completely forgiven them, he had been able to see God's bigger picture.

Receiving forgiveness when the person has died

So often we have unresolved issues because the broken relationship cannot be reconciled as one of the persons has died.

One lady, Lucy, came to see me about her eating disorder. Towards the end of many sessions where she had learnt to feel the feelings rather than stuff them down with food - the Holy Spirit gently led her back to think again about her mother who had died some five years previously. Lucy had a 'less than' relationship with her mother. She would visit regularly but always left feeling guilty despite the fact her mother never pressurized her. It was during our prayer sessions that Lucy realized she withheld love. On the surface she was loving, kind and friendly but underneath she held back. She had unacknowledged anger towards her mother because she felt her mother bent towards her troublesome brother and powerful father. When she realized this she was truly sorry and confessed her anger and lack of love to God, but obviously was unable to mend the relationship with her mother. So she buried this difficulty, pragmatically deciding that given the circumstances she and her mother had done the best they could.

Then came God's gift. Lucy was praying that God would lead her into all truth and was meditating on a clear lake symbolizing her heart. (This was an exercise in the book *Open Door* by Joyce

Rupp[96]) when she saw in the lake, half buried, an ornament
which had been precious to her mother. Jesus took it out from
the lake and Lucy and Jesus sat on the lakeside with the
ornament. Lucy asked Jesus what this all meant and he replied,
'This symbolizes your mother's forgiveness.'

Good news stories of forgiveness

Remember, when we forgive we are no longer controlled
internally by that person or the event. If we continue to pray,
we will be able to see the good in the person, see them as God
sees them and see the bigger picture (Joseph), and we will be
able to act generously towards them.

*'Dear friends, never take revenge. Leave that to the
righteous anger of God. For the Scriptures say, "I will take
revenge; I will pay them back," says the LORD'.* (Romans 12:19)
Forgiveness releases God to work. Forgiveness can bring a
release of transforming power.

A friend of mine, Pat, tells the story of a life changing
incident one New Year's Eve. Her marriage was difficult and her

husband attempted to control her by emotional withdrawal, long silences and feeling too ill to attend social engagements if she had upset him during the day. God had been healing her and, although she found it difficult, she had started to go out without him if he felt 'unwell.' This particular New Year's Eve Pat was stoically preparing to go to a party alone and whilst getting ready prayed that God would help her. She then had the thought to look in her prayer journal for the last year. As she looked, she saw how so much of her journalling was about her husband (perfectly valid) but with no forgiveness prayers. She proceeded to go through all the entries with a red felt tip writing 'forgiven'. As she finished the last page her husband walked up the stairs claiming he did not feel so bad after all and was going to the party!

Forgiveness and the Assurance of Restoration

Andrew was a middle-aged recovering alcoholic whom I had seen in the past and was now doing well. He wanted an appointment because he was unable to travel abroad through fear both of travelling and of being away from home.

He arrived and was quite angry, mainly at himself and the 'years the locusts had eaten.' So we started to look at some of the issues that led to his fears which were in essence a mixture of claustrophobia (trapped on a plane) and separation anxiety and agoraphobia.

1. His mother was/is agoraphobic.

2. His birth had been difficult. There had been a long labour and I presumed he had been stuck in the birth canal.

3. He also remembered being locked in a cupboard as a toddler and being trapped in caves in the Lake District as a teenager when the guide got lost.

4. Andrew had his first panic attack aged 20 in Paris some 20 years previously where he was given medication to which he became addicted.

We realized that now he was sober how much had been masked, but also how God had healed many things. We prayed for God to heal the baby, the toddler and the teenager thereby setting Andrew the adult free. Whilst praying all this Andrew saw a picture of a frog saying, 'This will never work, you will never be free.' We asked God to show us what this was about and Andrew had the word 'ridicule.' On talking I discovered he had always been ridiculed, criticized, laughed at and blamed at home, so we started to ask God to release and heal him from the words. At this point the frog turned into a grasshopper. This reminded me of the spies reporting from the promised land. So I prayed for Andrew's identity to catch up with his healing. As you will remember in Numbers 13:33, the spies speak about feeling like grasshoppers against the giants. They believed how they felt. Their identity was still that of being slaves despite all God had done. I asked Andrew to forgive his parents and brother for all the ridicule. As he forgave the picture changed and what to him was a grasshopper became a locust and he saw what he knew to be Jesus' foot come down and squash it. We then looked up Joel 2: 25, 'restore the years the locusts have eaten' and saw that it is linked with 23, which are the rains for the crops described as tokens of God's forgiveness! So for Andrew, forgiveness released the assurance of restoration.

When one man forgives

There are many amazing stories of Christian forgiveness. For example, Corrie ten Boom and stories from South Africa. But forgiveness is also powerful for non-Christians.

In such cases forgiveness is not because that person wants to please God; not because bitterness grieves the Spirit; not because setting people free ensures a greater anointing. It is because he or she is better off physically and emotionally for forgiving, worse off for not forgiving.

I have chosen to write about a remarkable man, Eric Lomax, who wrote a book called the Railway Man. Eric Lomax was a Japanese prisoner of war who had always been interested in railways. As a prisoner, he was part of the building of the Burma railway and because of his hobby he drew sketches of this on scraps of paper. When these were found, the Japanese wrongly assumed he was a spy. The following is taken from an article written in the Sunday Times on 20 August 1995.

As happens so often with the victims of torture, the inside wounds of Lomax's beatings never healed, and for nearly fifty years the torture poisoned his life. He was incomplete, haunted, trapped in an awful loneliness, internalizing his agony and nursing a fierce hatred.

The urge for revenge against the little Japanese interpreter Takahashi, who had been present at his ordeal was particularly acute. 'Although I could not have admitted it, I was still fighting the war in all those years of peace,' Lomax writes.

Stricken by conscience over his role in Lomax's torture and over Japanese militarism and atrocities, Takahashi had devoted much of his life to making up for the Japanese army's barbarity. Over the intervening years, he had built a peace temple near the railway and regularly made reconciliation visits to it, walking down, since 1945, a not totally dissimilar road of hurt and self examination to that of his victim.

Finally they met and the encounter was close to a spiritual experience; later, in Japan, Lomax found room in his heart to pardon Takahashi and wrote to him a personal letter of forgiveness. In ending his hate of his interrogator he became alive again.

In September 1998 I found this report in the newspaper. Eric Lomax accepted an invitation to have dinner in the same room as the Emperor and Empress of Japan and he was quoted as saying, 'I have proved for myself that remembering is not enough if it simply hardens the hate - the hating has to stop.'

When a country forgives

I think it would be impossible to write a chapter on forgiveness without mentioning South Africa. Professor Washington A. J. Okumu writes:

> Some of us who have been involved in the practical mediation of these conflicts have come to the stark realization that nations need to *forgive* each other for their past exploitation and suppression of their weaker neighbours just as much as individuals need to do.

American philosopher George Santayana once said, those who cannot remember the past are condemned to repeat it.

We must, therefore, learn to forgive even if we don't forget. Nelson Mandela is perhaps the best example in the twentieth century of a man who has taught us how to forgive. After twenty-seven years of political incarceration - the longest serving political prisoner in the world - he emerged unscathed and told his people to forgive their former white oppressors and instead fix their attention on the future: on building a new united nation. In spite of the devastating trauma of apartheid, Mandela chose the path of forgiveness and reconciliation rather than the policy of revenge and vindictiveness. The world had expected that the most ghastly bloodbath would overwhelm South Africa. This did not happen. Then the world thought that once a democratically elected government was in place with Mandela installed as its first black President, those who for so long had been denied their rights - whose dignity had been trodden underfoot, callously and without compunction - would go on the rampage, unleashing an orgy of revenge and retribution that would devastate their common motherland. But this did not happen either. South Africans managed an extraordinary, reasonably peaceful transition from the awfulness of repression to the relative stability of a non-racial democratic political dispensation. They had perhaps surprised even themselves at first by how much equanimity they had shown as some of the gory details of the past were rehearsed later in the Truth and Reconciliation Commission. It was a phenomenon that the world could not dismiss as insignificant. I am grateful to God who enabled me to play a role in that reconciliation and forgiving process, which saw the holding of peaceful and democratic elections in April 1994 and the avoidance of a major ethnic and racial war.

Nelson Mandela has been asked many times how he emerged from all those years in prison without being bitter. His reply is simple: 'Bitterness only hurts oneself.' The thing is, however, many who are bitter fully realize this, yet they still can't forgive. They know in their heads - rationally - that this bitterness is self-impoverishing. But they keep on doing it, feeling bitter. How did Nelson Mandela make this transition? The answer is in his words to President Bill Clinton: 'If you hate you will give them your heart and mind. Don't give those two things away.'[97]

Is forgiveness selfish?

There are many philosophical conversations concerning this question. Given the extreme benefits of forgiveness the view is expressed that you are looking after your own interests when you forgive. It is therefore ultimately selfish.

On the other hand, when you consider how difficult forgiveness is and how it flies in the face of our view of justice when we say 'let that person go unpunished' we see how totally unselfish it is.

My view is that it is simultaneously both, but there is a deeper issue, that of obedience.

'Make allowance for each other's faults, and forgive anyone who offends you. Remember, the Lord forgave you, so you must forgive others.' (Colossians 3:13 NLT)

Henri Nouwen writes:

It is freeing to become aware that we do not have to be victims of our past and can learn new ways of responding. But there is a step beyond this recognition. It is the step of forgiveness. Forgiveness is love practiced among people who love poorly. It sets us free without wanting anything in return.[98]

7

Genesis 1:26 NIV - *Then God said, "Let us make man in our own image, in our likeness, and let them rule over the fish of the sea and the birds of the air, over the livestock, over all the earth, and over all the creatures that move along the ground."*

The aim of God in history is the creation of an all-inclusive community of loving persons, with God himself at the very centre of this community as its prime sustainer and most glorious inhabitant. The bible traces the formation of this community from the creation of the Garden of Eden all the way to the new heaven and new earth. God not only creates, He continues to breathe His creativity into this living, pulsating universe. Human beings reflect that same creativity and the divine intent was that human beings should take responsibility for the earth and build community. God's intention for us all is to recognize that living to the full means cooperating with a God-shaped and God-filled reality.

Genesis begins with God speaking, using words to create a foundation that is solid and true. This foundation is brought to life when Jesus concludes His most famous teaching by telling us that there are two ways to go about our lives. We can build on sand or we can build on rock. No matter how wonderfully we build, if we build on sand it will fall to pieces like a house of cards. We need to learn to build on what is already there, on the rock. We are unfinished, somewhere between the blueprint and the final polish. However, we are no longer wandering exiles but quoting from The Message in Ephesians 2: *'This kingdom of faith is now your home country. You belong here, with as much right to the name Christian as anyone.'*

This home-build is both individual and in community. We need to be active participants in our own growth and this cannot take place in isolation. We are neurologically wired with the need to connect. God created us as relational beings. Particularly when we are coming out of shame and hiding, finding healthy relationships is not always straightforward. We need to look for a group of people, or a couple of friends who are committed to becoming all God wants them to be and are happy for us to join them.

EQUAL EXCHANGE

It's fine to have a therapist/prayer counsellor but our friendships and groups need to be on an 'equal exchange' basis.

'Choosing authenticity is not an easy choice.' E. E. Cummings wrote: 'To be nobody-but-yourself in a world which is doing its best night and day to make you everybody but yourself - means to fight the hardest battle which any human can fight - and never stop fighting.'[99]

Having to fight to stay real requires a lot of courage.

So often we join groups where we are seen as the 'project' or the 'less than' one. Some groups just leave us feeling cold and unconnected to God or undermined by their apparent ability to experience close relationship with God. When we are coming from a place of shame and hiding we can sometimes be so anxious for our own growth that we lack wisdom, effectively committing 'emotional striptease' in our quest for authenticity. Sitting in your swimsuit with everyone else in raincoats is not comfortable and not a good idea! We need to take small risks in vulnerability to begin with. Committing ourselves to openness needs to be with those who can handle honesty. Otherwise the group becomes solution-based, critical, defensive or 'parental'. This hurts us and does not necessarily lead to growth.

ATTRIBUTES OF A HEALTHY GROUP

A loving track record

James 2:15-17: '*Suppose there are brothers or sisters who need clothes and don't have enough to eat. What good is there in your saying to them, "God bless you! Keep warm and eat well!" - if you don't give them the necessities of life? So it is with faith: if it is alone and includes no actions, then it is dead.*'

We need to immerse ourselves in a group that inspires God honouring action. The first time I was planning a trip to a developing country I spoke with an ex-missionary and to the group I belonged to. We agreed there was nothing I could do on the big scale but I could make a difference to the people I met individually. We came up with the idea of tipping according to UK standards. This meant when the taxi driver asked for 50p for a journey that would have cost £5 in the UK, I gave him £5. By the end of the fortnight I was tempted to abandon this as the people with me thought I was extravagant but, remembering my group I wanted my 'walk' to match my 'talk.'

Ability to accept imperfections

Romans 12:9-10: '*Love must be completely sincere. Hate what is evil; hold on to what is good. Love one another warmly as Christian brothers and sisters, and be eager to show respect for one another.*'

Proverbs 19:11: '*A man's wisdom gives him patience: it is to his glory to overlook an offence.*'

Matthew 7:3: '*Why do you look at the speck of dust in your brother's eye and pay no attention to the plank in your own eye'!?*

The 'plank' in us causes 'poor eyesight' like the splinter of glass mirror in '*The Snow Queen'* or the 'dust of this world.' What this plank does is to magnify the speck of dust in the other person's eye whilst simultaneously blinding us to our own faults. Compassion for ourselves and others is of vital antidote to a harmful judgemental atmosphere. The more we are aware of our own unhealed areas or weakness and the more prepared we are to 'self-reveal' the more potential there is for growth and support.

Able to admit suffering

2 Corinthians 1:4: '*He helps us in all our troubles, so that we are able to help others who have all kinds of troubles, using the same help that we ourselves have received from God.*'

As I have written earlier, when we come from families who see needs and 'things going wrong' as shaming signs of weakness, it is difficult to be honest. I am sometimes asked to do some schools or retreats for various missionary societies. Very often, during private prayer times with people, I will hear of children's struggles, hating their boarding school, or from missionaries needing wisdom as to whether they should go come home to ailing, ageing parents and other difficulties. Yet when there is a time for 'sharing for prayer' within their groups, none of this is mentioned. The focus rather is on the work and the needs of the people they are serving. I do not fully understand why this is but I am sure it is not healthy.

A combination of truth, grace and faith

Truth and Grace - Ephesians 4:15: *'Instead, by speaking the truth in a spirit of love, we must grow up in every way to Christ, who is the head.'*

Faith - Philippians 1:6: *'And so I am sure that God, who began this good work in you, will carry it on until it is finished on the Day of Christ Jesus.'*

We need a combination of all three within a group. Graceless truth leads to "You should....", "You ought to.....", judgemental language and attitude, whereas truthless grace is statements such as, "Well, as long as you are happy....." or "Provided it doesn't hurt anyone."

As well as a good balance of truth and grace we need faith for change, the expectation that God loves us and because we are His masterpieces he will transform us.

People who help you grow good fruit

Matthew 7:17-20: *'A healthy tree bears good fruit, but a poor tree bears bad fruit. A healthy tree cannot bear bad fruit, and a poor tree cannot bear good fruit. And any tree that does not bear good fruit is cut down and thrown in the fire. So then, you will know the false prophets by what they do.'*

Does your group help you feel more loving? Do you feel closer to God and more confident to become all God intends you to be? That's what 'good fruit' is like.

I have belonged to a women's group for about thirty years. The following principles are what we think provides a supportive group.

A safe group

We offer hospitality, which means a 'healing shelter.' The meeting begins when two people have arrived, so two or three women talking in the kitchen, making tea and coffee is the beginning of the meeting, because relationships are the most important aspect. The focus isn't the formal teaching, though we always have bible teaching, the focus is being together. Because of this, unlike most of the church groups, we do not meet just in term-time; we meet every week because we want to. In the past, when we had a lot of school aged children, often one of the young girls home from university would offer to play with the children and look after them in another room or the garden.

It has to be safe. One lady, having just recovered from chemotherapy, took her wig off for us to see if the short hair looked okay. The group was where she could be vulnerable and experiment. Another lady used to come and sit and cry week after week. She then said one day, 'It's the only place I have to cry.'

A self revealing group

It can be a fairly large group, sometimes as many as twenty, but this doesn't ever seem to hinder the honesty. This is partly because those of us who lead the group are committed to self revealing. I am honest about my worries. I have cried when bad things have happened, I have chosen to not pretend when life isn't going well. We have decided as a group to be authentic, which means using straightforward, non-religious, language.

A Scripture based group

Discussion goes backwards and forwards over many topics but we also look to see what the bible says. Sometimes we study a book, sometimes certain subjects such as praise, forgiveness or faith. On one occasion we spent a few months looking at the Nicene Creed and recently spent nearly a year studying Romans 12.

A spirit-led group

We expect to pray for each other's physical healing, and to receive, for example, pictures from God for ourselves and for each other. Once we were praying for a lady in the church who didn't belong to the group but was a friend of a member, Lillian. Lillian's friend was desperate having had some late miscarriages. One night Lillian heard God say, "She will have a boy and call him Samuel" and Lillian told a few of us in the group. We kept quiet and continued to pray. The young lady became pregnant and whilst giving birth God said to her, "Call him Samuel"!

A group where sin can be confessed

It is essential for everyone to know that the group is safe so that they are able to reveal and confess. This means that there has to be a high degree of confidentiality. Of course we let each other down, but I can only think of two occasions where what was meant to be a 'group affair' i.e. confidential to the group, was gossiped about outside. On both occasions we were able to talk about it within the group and the person involved was able to say sorry. Safety also means we do not gossip *within* the group. There is no talking about the church or the leadership in a critical way, no judging, and an attempt to keep advice-giving to the minimum. Instead, we pray for each other.

A group that is secure, not separate from the church

We do not all belong to the same church. I however, and on the staff at All Saints Woodford Wells and so the group is within the church and is part of a 'cluster.' (For those not used to jargon, a cluster is a larger group of small groups). This also means that people during the rest of the week can meet and pray for each other and serve the church in various ways together, and this all happens in a free, 'organic' way. None of this needs the permission of the group leader.

A group that gives space

For me, a supportive group offers intimate fellowship, love and encouragement. This always leads, I believe, to space to grow, be transformed and to continue 'becoming.' Aesop's fable, 'The Wind and the Sun' encapsulates this well.

'The Wind and the Sun were disputing which was the stronger. Suddenly they saw a traveller coming down the road, and the Sun said: "I see a way to decide our dispute. Whichever of us can cause that traveller to take off his cloak shall be regarded as the stronger. You begin." So the Sun retired behind a cloud, and the Wind began to blow as hard as it could upon the traveller. But the harder he blew the more closely did the traveller wrap his cloak round him, till at last the Wind had to give up in despair. Then the Sun came out and shone in all his glory upon the traveller, who soon found it too hot to walk with his cloak on.'

Personal spiritual fitness

Someone who has spiritual personal wholeness manifests peace. When we are at peace within ourselves we feel 'at home' and fit snugly into God's design for us. We have a settled assurance of 'Christ within, the hope of Glory.' (Colossians 1:27). We desire to become all that God has called us to be, not because we fear failure in the world but because we know God's plans for us bring life in all its fullness.

Developing spiritual fitness is just like sports or music; anyone can join in, but the more we practise, the freer we are. We aren't dancing whilst we are learning steps. God gifts us but we need to practise. As children, our parents may have given us a bicycle as a gift but unless we learned to ride it, the present wasn't really received. A practised and free life is what God offers us or, to put it another way, the goal of human life should be to 'Glorify God and enjoy Him forever.'

I list below some of the spiritual 'fitness' principles we discovered in our group, not that any of us think we have 'arrived', but we have all found these helpful.

1. To let God love me

We may think about our relationship with God as one in which we have to perform, initiate and shape the relationship, whereas all the time God is saying such things as, 'Let me love you', Surrender to my love', 'Trust me', 'You belong to me'. Our responsibility in the relationship is to listen to and receive His love 'talk/song' to us.

2. God is in control

Nothing need happen to me that God does not allow. I awoke one morning to this sentence and thought it was so amazing I had better check it out! I asked the curate's wife, who lived opposite me, what she thought and she said she thought it was 'theologically sound.' 'Sound', I thought, 'It's amazing'!

It did not mean I would only experience good things. I knew Satan would do everything he could to turn me away from God and have me believe I was isolated and separate from God. I also knew Jesus had the ultimate victory. I knew there was sin - both mine and that of others - but I also knew the power of confession and deliverance.

I knew there was also my unhealed self, not necessarily sinful in the narrow sense of the word, but prone to sabotaging all that God had for me. This was usually because of an overwhelming desire for people to like me and a fear of doing anything that would jeopardise this.

I knew, then, that this did not mean I would not suffer but I also knew that God would always be with me. What followed was an intense spiritual experience. For three days the presence of Jesus was more real than any person or event. I lived in what I can only describe as a bubble. I called it 'Divine objectivity.'[100]

3. Develop a hunger for God

When we don't have a hunger for God we end up striving for more but looking in the wrong direction. This is why gluttony is a deadly sin: it is an appetite suppressant. Figuratively, full stomachs (be it food, drinking, fantasy, restless activity) cause jaded palates, they take the edge off our spiritual hunger and thirst. We end up with a 'small stomach' for spiritual food. We need to pray, 'Increase my capacity to receive from You, and make me hungry'.

For a couple of years I would read, 'As a dear pants for living water so my soul longs after you' and confess 'I am not like that

- make me thirsty, create thirst in me'. As we learn to hunger for God we will find we also hungering for social justice as well as for the beauty of God in nature and art. We need to learn how to make time to appreciate and receive all that God has for us. We need to cultivate the ability to enjoy and participate in creativity.

4. To continue to practise confession and forgiveness

One of the keys we have found to living in peace with one another in our group is to choose not to take offence, to focus on taking responsibility for ourselves, for the way we speak and behave, whilst believing the best of each other. This means we are the first to say, 'I am sorry' and to privately forgive those who have upset us whilst asking God to heal the wounds.

5. The virtue of hope

Hope is a gift. It becomes a virtue as we practise. We learn that Christian hope is neither wishful thinking nor is it an emotion like a warm feeling of optimism. Christian hope is not based on an idealised future prospect, but on a person - Jesus - who has proved Himself trustworthy.

6. Learning to desire

Jesus asks us, 'What do you want?' It is vital we get in touch with our heart's desires, not the 'oughts and shoulds' of religion. (For more insight read chapter 4 of Father Matters). We become fully alive people as we desire. God teaches us who we are by revealing to us what we want. One of the most difficult steps in my Christian walk was to get in touch with my desires.

7. Setting boundaries

This was a painful step for me but carried on from my desire list. The second desire on my list had been to let my 'yes' be 'yes' and my 'no' be 'no.' (James 5:12). The 'yes' was no problem to me but I had enormous difficulty with saying 'no' to people. This was because I was desperate to fit in, wanted to be perfect and I misunderstood what was meant by 'Christian service'. This led to feeling that no-one really liked me for who I was, only for what I could do for them.

When we fail to set boundaries and hold people accountable we feel used and mistreated. This failure is dangerous to the well-being of the relationships because we either blame ourselves and try harder or become full of (normally unspoken) self-righteous anger and resentment. Some of us, of course, need to start saying 'Yes' and come out from our self-built fortresses. The problem is that when we don't care at all what people think, and we are immune to hurt, we are also ineffective at connecting. Living life to the full can only take place in relationships because that is God's intention.

8. Learning to trust

The more we are able to trust in the faithfulness of God and His promises to us, the less likely we will be to worry. Trusting in His character enables us to let go of the trivia of life and to cooperate with His 'unforced rhythms of grace'. Worry and trust are like oil and water, they cannot coexist.

9. Living in the now

Matthew 6:34: '*Therefore, do not worry about tomorrow, for tomorrow will worry about itself. Each day has enough trouble of its own.*'

In order to experience the 'eternal now' we need to stop rehearsing future conversations in our heads, tear up our 'to do' lists, our indefinable future plans and start living today.'

We also need to learn to not look back. God can redeem our past, restoring the pain and loss of past years. Our worries, regret and remorse can achieve nothing. It is a *daily* manna, *daily* bread that we need. The present moment is the only moment in which we can practise the presence of Jesus. The place 'He is' is here now. Living in the now helps us to touch and experience eternity, which of course is timeless, or where all time is present.

10. Be who God made you to be

We know God is good. What is more, we know God is good to us! One of the difficulties in becoming all that God has called us to be, and experiencing abundant life, is thinking small. We try to fit the life of Christ into our lives and then try to make more room for God. Yet the more we think like this, the more rules, 'oughts' and 'shoulds' clutter our lives. Instead of becoming large we find ourselves feeling claustrophobic and diminished. God is not in space - space is in God. In order to 'become' we must learn to come out of hiding, and even when we are hurting, and wanting to isolate, we need to continue to meet with others. Coming out of hiding means we have to stop pretending and burying all our insecurities under a mound of achievements.

Life, as John Lennon wrote, is what happens when you are busy making other plans. Living in the, 'when I get there', 'somewhere over the rainbow', robs us of the 'joy of now.'

Mark Twain wrote, '*Dance like no-one is watching, sing like no-one is listening, love like you've never been hurt and live like it's heaven on earth.*'

And this, we need to practice in our everyday, ordinary lives. Ordinary is good. So often we don't know this. Brené Brown writes:

> "We seem to measure the value of people's contributions (and sometimes their entire lives) by their level of public recognition. In other words, worth is measured by fame and fortune. Our culture is quick to dismiss quiet, ordinary, hard-working men and women. In many instances, we equate *ordinary* with *boring* or, even more dangerous, *ordinary* has become synonymous with *meaningless.*"[101]

But our ordinary is transformed not by fame and fortune but by seeing God in our everyday, ordinary. God is with us.

The more we live in this and practise gratitude, the more enjoyable life is and the freer we become. When we are secure in God's love for us we can lose ourselves because we know we will get ourselves back!

We need to place our lives in the hands of God and trust what those hands will do. The goal of human life needs to be to glorify God and enjoy Him forever.

'To glorify God is to do these things and by doing them to make God's intentions in the world more luminous and God's reputation more lustrous. To enjoy God for ever is to cultivate a taste for this project, to become more and more the sort of person for whom eternal life with God would be sheer heaven.'[102]

END NOTES

Chapter 1

1. C. S. Lewis, *Miracles*

2. G. K. Chesterton, *The Paradoxes of Christianity*

3. C. S. Lewis, The Weight of Glory

4. St. Augustine, *Confessions of St. Augustine of Hippo*

5. C. S. Lewis, *Weight of Glory*

6. J. Milton, *Paradise Lost*

7. Curt Thompson, *Anatomy of the Soul.* I have borrowed and used extensively his insights throughout his story of Adam and Eve

8. A. W. Tozer, *Experiencing the Presence of God*

9. Curt Thompson, *Anatomy of the Soul*

10. For more information on the 'Dove' see Chapter 5 of Mother Matters

11. C. S. Lewis, *Mere Christianity*

12. I have taken this connection between Jesus baptism and creation from Tim Kellor's book *King's Cross*

Chapter 2

13. Mark Biddle, *Missing the Mark: Sin and its Consequences in Biblical Theology* quoted in Alan Mains article *Understanding Sin, Recognising Shame*

14. Stephen Pattison, *Shame: Theory, Therapy, Theology*

15. Silvan S. Tomkins, quoted in Gershen Kaufman, *The Psychology of Shame: Theory and Treatment of Shame-Based Syndromes*

16. Andy Comiskey, *Strength in Weakness*

17. Gershen Kaufman, *Shame: The Power of Caring*

18. C. S. Lewis, *The Business of Heaven Daily Readings*

19. Barbara Wood, *Children of Alcoholism: The Struggle for Self and Intimacy in Adult Life*

20. Alice Miller, *For Your Own Good*

21. Gershen Kaufman, *The Psychology of Shame*

22. Brennan Manning, *A Stranger to Self-Hatred*

23. For more on Separation Anxiety see Mother Matters chapter 2.

24. Adaptation of a prayer by Mary Hancock

Chapter 3

25. This was read at a conference by Gerard Hughes and is by Oriah Mountain Dreamer

26. Curt Thompson, *Anatomy of the Soul*

27. Dr John Townsend, *Hiding from Love* expands on this with a fictional account of hiding called 'Jenny's Story'.

28. John Stasi Eldredge, *Love and War*

29. Leanne Payne, *Restoring the Christian Soul*

30. C. S. Lewis, *Surprised by Joy*

31. Bob George, *Classic Christianity - The Story*

32. Adapted from a sermon by Ray Dillard quoted in Tim Kellor's *King's Cross*

33. This is written about in more detail in Father Matters

34. Bob George, *Classic Christianity*

35. James Proctor, *It Is Finished*

36. Andy Comiskey, Desert Stream Ministries - www.desertstream.org

37. Dallas Willard, *Spirit of the Disciplines*

38. Dr John Townsend, *Hiding from Love*

Chapter 4

39. Scott Morgan Peck, *A Road Less Travelled*

40. Rick Richardson, *Experiencing Healing* p10

41. This is adapted from an article by Dr Elisha Goldstein, *Why Bad Things Happen to Good People*

42. This is adapted from an article by Dr Bob Ekblad in the New Wine Magazine, Autumn 2011

43. Thomas A. Kempis, *The Day of Eternity and of the Distresses of this Life*

44. Gerald Sitser, *Way of Life* (Earliest Usage of a now common term)

45. Cornelius Plantinga Jnr, *Not the Way it's Supposed to be: A Breviary of Sin*

46. Victor Hugo, *The Letters of Victor Hugo: From Exile and After the Fall of the Empire*

47. Taken from an article by Anne Coles

48. Benjamin Franklin, *Poor Richard's Almanac*

49. C. S. Lewis, *Chronicles of Narnia: The Lion, the Witch and the Wardrobe*

50. C. S. Lewis, *Yours Jack: The Inspirational Letters*

51. The idea of comparing Jonah with St. Patrick is taken from the Renovaré Bible

52. Brother Francis is a children's palliative care nurse in Scotland

53. Aleksandr Solzhenitsyn, *The Gulag Archipelago*

54. Dallas Willard, *Spiritual Formation and the Warfare Between the Flesh and the Human Spirit*

55. Victor Frankl, *Man's Search for Meaning*

56. Martin Luther King (taken from a speech in Memorial Park, Seattle)

57. Bob Ekblad, *Musings on Mary and Martha*

58. Eugene Peterson, *Living the Message*

Chapter 5

59. C. S. Lewis, *Reflections on the Psalms*

60. Tony Campolo, *The Kingdom of God is a Party*

61. Mark Twain, *Following the Equator*

62. Clay McLean - www.mcleanministries.org

63. Martin Luther King quoted in Edith Simon Luther, *Alive* and Philip Yancey, *Rumours of Another World*

64. C. S. Lewis, *Mere Christianity*

65. Cornelius Platinga Jnr, *Not the Way it's Supposed to be: A Breviary of Sin*

66. C.S. Lewis, *Mere Christianity*

67. Second Helvetic Confession was first published in Germany in 1564. This document expressed the common belief of the Reformed Churches

68. For more on the dangers of fantasy see Mother Matters Chapter 4

69. Herman Melville, *That Inscrutable Thing: Moby Dick*

70. Philip Yancey, *Rumours of Another World*

71. John Calvin: Institutes of the Christian Religion

72. Philip Yancey, *Rumours of Another World*

73. R. T. Kendall, *Total Forgiveness*

74. Keith Miller, *The Secret Life of the Soul*

75. Dietrich Bonhoeffer, *The Works of Dietrich BonHoeffer Vol 5*

76. Philip Yancey, *Rumours of Another World*

77. Francois Fenlon quoted in A. W. Tozer, *Experiencing the Presence of God*

78. A. W. Tozer, *Experiencing the Presence of God*

79. I have taken the connection between knowing we have changed and this story from R.T. Kendall, *Total Forgiveness*

80. Perry D. LeFevre Ed., *The Prayers of Kierkegaard*

81. Richard Haefleur, *Will Daylight Come*

Chapter 6

82. Abbot Macarius quoted in Paul Russell, *Making Your Life A Christian Life: The Desert Fathers and St Francis of Assisi 2009. p83*

83. George MacDonald, *Unspoken Sermons*

84. William Blake, prologue from *The Gates of Paradise*

85. Ed Hallowell M.D Ed.D, a child and adult psychiatrist and best selling author

86. More details can be found in R.T. Kendall, *Total Forgiveness*

87. Clay McLean - www.mcleanministries.org

88. Philip Yancey, *What's So Amazing About Grace?*

89. Lewis B. Smedes, *Forgive and Forget: Healing the Hurts We Don't Deserve*

90. For more on Separation Anxiety see Lin Button, *Mother Matters*

91. For more on Control and Boundary Setting see Lin Button, *Father Matters*

92. Sigmund Freud, *The Interpretation of Dreams*

93. Professor C. Kilby, *A Mind Awake: An Anthology of C. S. Lewis*. Although often quoted it is not accurate but rather a culmination of several quotes. The exact quote is, "We may need to forgive our brother 70x7, not only for 490 offences but for one offence."

94. Reverend Charles Frederic Aked, *Bartlett's Familiar Quotations*. Attributed to Edmund Burke in 1921 but thought to have been changed to its current form - "For evil men to accomplish their purpose it is only necessary that good men should do nothing."

95. Lin Button, *Mother Matters*

96. Joyce Rupp, *Open Door.* Contains many useful meditations.

97. R. T. Kendall, *Total Forgiveness.* (Please see for a fuller version)

98. Henri Nouwen, *The Return of the Prodigal Son*

Chapter 7

99. E. E. Cummings, *A Miscellany: A Poet's Advice to Students*. Humanistic Psychology Vol 12, No 2. 1972

100. I had heard Leanne Payne use this expression and I think my experience defined it.

101. Brené Brown, *The Gift of Imperfection*

102. Cornelius Plantinga, *Not the Way Its Supposed To Be: A Breviary of Sin*

Testimonies from 'Father Matters'.

"After praying for the desire of my heart I received a physical healing."

"I gave Father Matters to my sister-in-law who recommitted her life to Jesus."

To contact the author or for more information:

Dr Lin Button
PO Box 500
Woodford Green
Essex
IG8 0YB

Tel: 020 8504 3966
E-mail: linbutton@healingprayerschool.org

Or visit the website at:

www.healingprayerschool.org

Please include your testimony or help received from this book when you write. Prayer requests are welcome.